Parents

quick & easy

Kid-Friendly Meals

WILEY

John Wiley & Sons, Inc.

Library of Congress Cataloging-in-Publication Data:

Parents quick and easy kid-friendly meals / Parents Magazine

    p. cm.

    Includes index.

    ISBN 978-1-118-17360-2 (pbk.); ISBN 978-1-118-26057-9 (ebook); ISBN 978-1-118-26059-3 (ebook); ISBN 978-1-118-26063-0 (ebook)

    1. Quick and easy cooking. 2. Children--Nutrition. 3. Cookbooks. I. Parents Magazine Enterprises.

    TX833.5.P38 2012

    641.5'55--dc23

               2011048143

Printed in the United States of America

Parents® *Quick & Easy Kid-Friendly Meals*

Editor-in-Chief: Dana Points

Executive Editor: Chandra Turner

Creative Director: Andrea Amadio

Managing Editor: Kathleen Krems

Associate Managing Editor: Michaela Garibaldi

Contributing Food and Nutrition Editor: Karen Cicero

Test Kitchen Project Manager: Colleen Weeden

John Wiley & Sons, Inc.

Publisher: Natalie Chapman

Associate Publisher: Jessica Goodman

Senior Editor: Linda Ingroia

Production Director: Diana Cisek

Production Editor: Marina Padakis Lowry

Manufacturing Manager: Tom Hyland

Waterbury Publications, Inc.

Editors: Lisa Kingsley, Tricia Bergman, Mary Williams

Design Director: Ken Carlson

Associate Design Directors: Doug Samuelson, Bruce Yang

Production Assistant: Mindy Samuelson

Cover photos:

Front: Top, from left: Josh Titus, Cheryl Zibisky, Miki Duisterhof; **Middle:** Rita Maas; **Bottom, from left:** Lucy Schaeffer, Frances Janisch, David Prince; **Spine:** Alison Miksch; **Back: Top, from left:** Frances Janisch, Alison Miksch, Paula Hible; **Bottom, from left:** Rita Maas, Alison Miksch, Monica Buck

Welcome to Our Kitchen!

What parent doesn't feel pressured these days to deliver three square meals made fresh and with love? Yet between work and household chores and feeling the need to watch my family's waistlines, our nutrient intake, *and* our pennies, I sometimes start to dread figuring out dinner and I am guessing that if you've picked up this book, you do too.

That's where these recipes come in — 125 of them, all kitchen-tested and measuring up to the high standards of *Parents* where food is concerned. Whether you're a kitchen newbie looking for guidance now that you're feeding a toddler, or a seasoned cook simply seeking fresh ideas, you'll find plenty of inspiration in these pages. We strive to help readers raise healthy, adventurous eaters by giving moms (and more than a few dads) all the tips and tools you need to prepare fast, wallet-friendly meals that appeal to the entire family. Our goal is for your whole gang to enjoy the same meal—you shouldn't need to prepare a separate kiddie dinner. All our recipes include nutritional information, in case you're watching your calories or your calcium, for example, and our balanced, everything-in-moderation approach means you can make room for treats, as well as our memorable desserts.

Speaking of treats, don't miss out on the extra food features on our website. Visit **parents.com/food** and sign up for our weekly newsletter, and you'll get a fresh infusion of food ideas delivered to your inbox just when you're hungry for inspiration.

Now turn to any page in this book and try making something new for your family today!

Dana

Dana Points
Editor-in-Chief

7 Healthy Eating Habits for Families

If feeding your family has you seriously stressed, you'll love this list the editors at *Parents* cooked up. Nutrition experts helped us sort through all the confusing food news, and boiled down what's most important to keep in mind when planning meals for your child—and yourself. Just follow these simple steps to healthy, less-hectic meals.

1. Go for Whole Grains. At least half of your kid's grain servings should be the unrefined type—like whole wheat, oats, and brown rice—because they pack more vitamin E, fiber, and magnesium than their more processed counterparts. So if your kid balks about having his turkey and cheese sandwich on anything else than his favorite white bread, don't fight that battle. Just make sure he has whole grains at other meals, like oatmeal for breakfast and whole-grain tortilla chips at snack time.

2. Pick Your Protein. Your child needs protein to grow—it helps build and repair every tissue in the body. But a little goes a long way. Simply include one protein-rich food three times a day—say, an egg at breakfast, a couple tablespoons of hummus for a snack, and a small piece of chicken at dinner—and that's plenty.

3. Find the Right Fat. All kinds of fats will help your kid grow, transport vitamins through the body, and provide vitamin E. But unsaturated fat is much better for your kid's heart than the saturated type. Serve your child low-fat dairy foods and lean meat (to get the food's benefits without saturated fat) and work unsaturated fat into your family's diet by cooking with olive or canola oil instead of butter, and having nuts, avocados, or olives a couple times a week. (Just make sure the nuts are ground and nut butters are thinly spread for kids under age 4.)

4. Watch the Sodium. You may not add much salt to your family's meals, but if you bought any packaged ingredients, the manufacturers probably have. Look for low-sodium or no-salt-added versions of foods you cook with often, like chicken stock, canned beans, and tomato sauce. When your child overdoes it on sodium, he's more at risk for high-blood pressure, which affects an alarming 1 in 20 kids.

5. Pour Responsibly. Some kids consume more calories from beverages than food at a meal, putting them at risk for being overweight. Your child needs low-fat milk, but two to three cups a day is plenty, especially if she's eating other dairy foods like yogurt and cheese. Juice is optional, and children ages 1 to 6 shouldn't exceed 4 to 6 ounces of fruit juice daily, while older kids shouldn't go over 8 to 12 ounces. Once your kid has had enough milk for the day, switch to water. Let her squirt in the juice from a lemon wedge or orange slice to make it seem more fun.

6. Listen to His Tummy. Suggesting that your child "clean his plate" or "just have three more bites" will likely backfire, and encourage him to eat for reasons other than hunger. Rather, ask, "Are you full?" or "How does your tummy feel?"

7. Keep Trying. If your kid thinks broccoli is gross or seafood tastes, well, too fishy, don't give up. Sure, it's majorly annoying to have your kid turn her nose up at something you spent time cooking. But persistence pays off: Studies suggest that kids need to try some foods 15 to 20 times before they like the flavor.

8 breakfast

28 lunch

66 supper

162 snacks
& drinks

188 treats

breakfast

EGGS • GRAINS • FRUIT & YOGURT

Most kids **wake up hungry,** so they're not as picky at 6 a.m. as they are at 6 p.m. Use the morning meal to **introduce new foods** and flavors to your family's fussy eater.

Fast Frittata

If you can't find the flavored egg product used in this recipe, stir ⅓ cup salsa into a carton of the plain version.

INGREDIENTS

1 tablespoon vegetable oil

½ 20-ounce package refrigerated shredded hash brown potatoes (2½ cups)

Salt and pepper

4 ounces pre-cooked smoked turkey sausage, quartered lengthwise and sliced crosswise

1 carton (15 ounces) Egg Beaters Southwestern flavor

1 ounce Manchego or Parmesan cheese, finely shredded

MAKE IT

1 Heat oil on medium in a large ovenproof nonstick skillet. Add potatoes and sprinkle lightly with salt and pepper. Cook for 5 minutes or until the potatoes are lightly browned, stirring occasionally. Press potatoes into a uniform layer.

2 Top potatoes evenly with turkey sausage and egg. Cook, uncovered, for 5 minutes, occasionally tilting skillet and lifting frittata around the edges with a spatula to allow uncooked mixture to flow underneath.

3 Turn on broiler. Broil egg mixture 4 to 5 inches from the heat for 2 to 4 minutes, or until the top is set. Sprinkle frittata with cheese. Let stand 5 minutes before cutting. Makes 8 servings.

Nutrition per serving: 130 calories; 9g protein; 5g fat (2g saturated fat); 11g carbohydrate; 1g fiber; 64mg calcium; 1mg iron; 489mg sodium.

nutrition note

Both Manchego—a sheep's milk cheese from Spain—and Parmesan are aged cheeses. They're generally lower in fat than other types, and they have a slightly sharper flavor, too, so a little goes a long way. They're both good choices for encouraging healthful and adventurous eating.

Breakfast Over Easy

Not only are these egg dishes cute, but they're also packed with protein, which will keep your child going strong until it's lunchtime.

← Huevos Rancheros

What kid could resist tortilla chips for breakfast? This dish is healthy, too, with vitamin-rich eggs and fresh salsa.

MAKE IT

Scramble an egg and place it on a handful of baked tortilla chips. Sprinkle with 2 tablespoons reduced-fat shredded cheddar cheese and top with a spoonful of chunky tomato salsa. Makes 1 serving.

Nutrition per serving: 171 calories; 12g protein; 8g fat (3g saturated fat); 14g carbohydrate; 1g fiber; 179mg calcium; 1mg iron; 369mg sodium.

← Sunshine Eggs

These bright beauties are a different way to make eggs sunny side up. Kids will love breakfast out of an egg cup. It's simple for you yet special for them.

MAKE IT

Place an egg in a small pot and cover with cold water. Bring to a boil, remove from heat, cover, and let stand 16 minutes. Peel; cut in half, and sprinkle with a little bit of paprika or parsley. Serve in an egg cup. Makes 1 serving.

Nutrition per serving: 72 calories; 6g protein; 5g fat (2g saturated fat); 0g carbohydrate; 0g fiber; 27mg calcium; 1mg iron; 70mg sodium.

EGG-CELLENT EGGS

Yolks supply choline, a nutrient that helps a young child's brain and nervous system develop. Plus, eggs are loaded with iron, vitamin D, protein, and certain antioxidants that help protect your child's vision.

← Love Nest

Your kid will "heart" this version of the classic egg-in-a-hole breakfast treat.

MAKE IT

With a small heart-shaped cookie cutter, cut a hole in the center of a slice of whole-grain bread. Spread both sides lightly with margarine and place in a small pan on the stove top that has been heated on medium. Crack an egg into the hole and cook until almost set, 4 to 5 minutes. Carefully flip and continue cooking for another minute or two, until egg is completely set. Makes 1 serving.

Nutrition per serving: 138 calories; 10g protein; 7g fat (2g saturated fat); 10g carbohydrate; 3g fiber; 43mg calcium; 2mg iron; 178mg sodium.

German Pancake with Berries

Give the kids a job: Once this pancake cools, ask them to decorate it with berries.

INGREDIENTS

- 2 tablespoons butter
- 2 eggs
- ½ cup all-purpose flour
- ½ cup reduced-fat milk
- 1 tablespoon granulated sugar
- 1 teaspoon vanilla extract
- ¼ teaspoon salt
- 3 cups fresh blueberries, raspberries, blackberries, and sliced strawberries
- 2 tablespoons powdered sugar

MAKE IT

1 Heat oven to 400°F. Place butter in a 10-inch ovenproof skillet. Put the skillet in the oven for 3 to 5 minutes, or until butter melts. Whisk eggs in a bowl. Add flour, milk, granulated sugar, vanilla, and salt; whisk until the mixture is smooth. Immediately pour batter into the hot skillet. Bake for 20 to 25 minutes, or until puffed and browned.

2 Remove from the oven. The pancake will fall in the center as it cools. Top with berries and powdered sugar. Cut in six pieces and serve immediately. Makes 6 servings.

Nutrition per serving: 159 calories; 5g protein; 6g fat (3g saturated fat); 22g carbohydrate; 3g fiber; 47mg calcium; 1mg iron; 157mg sodium.

cooking fun

For a family outing, take your kids to a pick-your-own berry farm. They'll learn about how different kinds of berries grow, and how fresh fruit tastes and looks. When you get home, cool down with a smoothie. Toss the berries, milk or yogurt, and a splash of juice in the blender.

Pint-Size Pancakes & Waffles

These popular breakfast breads are packed with fruit—not soaked in butter and syrup—so they're healthy enough to eat every day. Even better: You can make any of them in less than 10 minutes.

← Tiny Waffle Tower

Kids will love eating these fruit-and-cream cheese-filled towers layer by layer. We used strawberries and bananas, but peaches and blueberries make a great combo too.

MAKE IT

Spread reduced-fat or fat-free strawberry cream cheese on two toasted mini waffles (we like Van's brand). Stack the waffles with sliced strawberries and bananas in between the layers. Place another waffle and a fanned-out strawberry on top. Makes 1 serving.

Nutrition per serving: 100 calories; 3g protein; 3g fat (1g saturated fat); 15g carbohydrate; 1g fiber; 62mg calcium; 1mg iron; 165mg sodium.

← Ricotta Cheese Pancakes

Ricotta cheese gives these pancakes a moist, tender texture—and an extra bone-building calcium and protein boost.

MAKE IT

In a medium bowl, mix 3 tablespoons whole-wheat flour, 2 teaspoons sugar, and 1 teaspoon baking powder. Stir in 1 beaten egg and ½ cup part-skim ricotta cheese. Fold in ¼ cup frozen raspberries. Pour about ¼ cup batter for each pancake onto hot griddle; cook for 2 to 3 minutes. Flip and cook for another minute or so until set. Makes 4 pancakes.

Nutrition per two-pancake serving: 184 calories; 12g protein; 8g fat (4g saturated fat); 18g carbohydrate; 2g fiber; 358mg calcium; 2mg iron; 294mg sodium.

GREAT GRAINS

Whether you purchase whole-grain waffles or pancakes or make your own, introducing your child to the nutty, hearty flavor of whole grains early in life will help shape his preferences—for the better.

← Letter-Perfect Waffles

Spell out your child's initials in blueberries in this clever breakfast treat, or better still, let him do it. What a tasty way to learn the ABCs!

MAKE IT

Cook two whole-grain frozen waffles according to the package directions. Arrange blueberries to make your child's initials. Sift a little powdered sugar on top. Makes 1 serving.

Nutrition per serving: 160 calories; 5g protein; 3g fat (1g saturated fat); 33g carbohydrate; 3g fiber; 101mg calcium; 4mg iron; 430mg sodium.

Chocolate-Hazelnut Pancakes with Raspberry Sauce

If you have a toddler in the house, tear pancakes into pieces and put a few teaspoons of sauce on her plate. Let her "paint" the pancakes with the sauce.

INGREDIENTS

Pancakes

- 1¼ cups all-purpose flour
- 2 teaspoons baking powder
- ¼ teaspoon salt
- ¼ cup chocolate-hazelnut spread
- 1 egg
- 3 tablespoons sugar, divided
- 1¼ cups low-fat milk
- Canola oil

Sauce

- 1 12-ounce package frozen raspberries
- ¼ cup cold water
- 1 tablespoon cornstarch

MAKE IT

1 Whisk together flour, baking powder, and salt. In another bowl, whisk chocolate-hazelnut spread, egg, 1 tablespoon sugar, and milk. Whisk milk mixture into flour mixture (it's okay if there are a few lumps).

2 Heat oil-coated skillet on medium. Pour in ¼ cup of batter. Cook 2 to 3 minutes. Turn when bubbles appear. Cook 1 to 2 minutes until brown on the bottom.

3 Put the raspberries and remaining sugar in a pan (break up berries with a spoon). Heat on medium until bubbly. Mix the water and cornstarch. Add to berry mixture. Stir and cook 2 minutes past when sauce thickens. Strain seeds if desired. Makes 10 pancakes and 1¾ cups sauce.

Nutrition per pancake with 1½ tablespoons sauce: 151 calories; 4g protein; 4g fat (1g saturated fat); 26g carbohydrate; 3g fiber; 117mg calcium; 1mg iron; 157mg sodium.

nutrition note

Be sure to use unsweetened frozen raspberries to prepare the sauce for these pancakes. Look at the ingredients list to make sure sugar, high-fructose corn syrup, honey, or brown rice syrup hasn't been added.

Banana-Quinoa Waffles with Mixed Berries

These waffles are so healthy that it's okay to drizzle real maple syrup on them.

INGREDIENTS

- ½ cup water
- ¼ cup quinoa
- 1⅔ cups white whole-wheat flour
- 2 tablespoons packed brown sugar
- 1 teaspoon baking powder
- ¼ teaspoon salt
- 1 cup mashed ripe banana
- 3 eggs, separated
- 4 tablespoons (½ stick) unsalted butter, melted
- 1½ cups fat-free milk
- 2 cups fresh berries (blueberries, raspberries, sliced strawberries)
- Maple syrup (if desired)

MAKE IT

1 In a small saucepan, bring the water to a boil. Stir in quinoa. Reduce heat, cover, and simmer for 10 to 12 minutes, until tender and liquid is absorbed. Remove from heat. Transfer to small bowl; chill 1 to 2 hours.

2 Preheat waffle iron, according to manufacturer's instructions. In a large bowl, combine flour, brown sugar, baking powder, and salt. In a medium bowl, combine cooked quinoa, banana, egg yolks, butter, and milk. Add to flour mixture; stir until combined.

3 In another medium bowl, beat egg whites until stiff. Fold in banana batter.

4 Add batter to waffle iron. Cook according to manufacturer's instructions. Top with berries and syrup, if desired. Makes 10 waffles.

Nutrition per waffle: 176 calories; 7g protein; 5g fat (3g saturated fat); 27g carbohydrate; 3g fiber; 95mg calcium; 1mg iron; 133mg sodium.

nutrition note

Wondering what quinoa (pronounced *KEEN-wa*) is? It's a healthy whole grain just like oats or barley except that it's a better source of protein. In fact its protein is as complete as milk, meat, and eggs. It also contains fiber, manganese, magnesium, folate, iron, and phosphorus. With a light nutty flavor, quinoa can be served as a hot breakfast cereal, in place of rice in rice pudding, or as a side dish.

Tasty Toast

There may be nothing more basic for breakfast than a piece of toast—but with these creative ideas, your child won't even notice that it's made with whole wheat, not white, bread.

← Checkerboard Toast

If your kid can't decide between peanut butter or Nutella, try this fun way to work in both.

MAKE IT

Cut the crust off a piece of whole-grain toast. Thinly spread opposite top and bottom squares with peanut butter and Nutella (chocolate-hazelnut spread) for a checkerboard effect. Makes 1 serving.

Nutrition per serving: 206 calories; 8g protein; 10g fat (1g saturated fat); 23g carbohydrate; 5g fiber; 24mg calcium; 1mg iron; 169mg sodium.

← Chocolate-Milk French Toast

Serve chocolate at breakfast, and your child will think you're the coolest mom in the world.

MAKE IT

Dunk 3 slices of whole-grain bread into a mixture of 1 beaten egg, ¼ cup low-fat chocolate milk, and a dash of vanilla extract and let bread soak up some liquid. Cook a few minutes on each side on a hot griddle. Cut slices in half and sprinkle with cocoa powder and cut each slice in half. Serve with pear slices. Makes 2 servings.

Nutrition per serving: 211 calories; 12g protein; 5g fat (1g saturated fat); 31g carbohydrate; 8g fiber; 84mg calcium; 2mg iron; 220mg sodium.

WE LOVE
WHOLE WHEAT

Whole-wheat bread has more fiber than the white stuff, so your kid won't beg you for a snack an hour later. It also packs more vitamin E, magnesium, and zinc because it's not as processed.

← Jigsaw Puzzle

If your kid needs a little motivation to eat before school, this is the breakfast for her.

MAKE IT

Spread a piece of whole-grain toast with 1 teaspoon softened butter. Cut the middle out of a slice with a small cookie cutter, like a star. Cut the rest with a knife. Place shaped center piece in the middle of a plate with remaining pieces all around it. Have your child put the puzzle back together before she eats. Makes 1 serving.

Nutrition per serving: 124 calories; 5g protein; 5g fat (2g saturated fat); 15g carbohydrate; 4g fiber; 21mg calcium; 1mg iron; 137mg sodium.

Blueberry Scones

For a special weekend breakfast, try these whole-grain scones that have half the calories and fat of bakery versions.

INGREDIENTS

- 1¼ cups all-purpose flour, plus extra for work surface
- ¾ cup whole-wheat flour
- 1 tablespoon granulated sugar
- 2 teaspoons baking powder
- ¼ teaspoon salt
- ½ cup low-fat milk, plus 2 teaspoons
- 3 tablespoons canola oil
- 1 egg
- ¾ cup fresh blueberries
- ½ cup powdered sugar

MAKE IT

1 Heat oven to 400°F and spray a baking sheet with olive oil. In a large bowl, combine the flours, sugar, baking powder, and salt. In a small bowl, combine ½ cup milk, the oil, and egg. Pour liquid mixture into the dry mixture. Mix to combine. Add blueberries.

2 Sprinkle additional flour on a cutting board and turn the dough over on it, then pat into an 8-inch circle. Score dough into 8 wedges, cutting just halfway through the dough. Bake 20 minutes; finish cutting wedges and place on a wire rack.

3 Once the scones are cool enough to touch, mix powdered sugar and 2 teaspoons milk. Drizzle over scones with a spoon. Makes 8 scones.

Nutrition per scone: 215 calories; 5g protein; 6g fat (1g saturated fat); 35g carbohydrate; 2g fiber; 50mg calcium; 2mg iron; 149mg sodium.

kitchen tip

Be sure not to overmix the dough after you've combined the dry and wet ingredients; doing so will make the scones tough.

Yummy Yogurt

These calcium-rich breakfasts may look like treats to your child—so keep it to yourself how healthy they really are.

← Mango Split

Make this with a perfectly ripe mango. You'll know it's ready when it feels plump and heavy for its size. The flesh should give slightly when pressed gently with your finger—and it should smell sweetly fragrant.

MAKE IT

Top a wedge of mango with ½ cup low-fat strawberry yogurt and sprinkle with 2 tablespoons shredded coconut. Makes 1 serving.

Nutrition per serving: 221 calories; 7g protein; 2g fat (1g saturated fat); 43g carbohydrate; 2g fiber; 197mg calcium; 1mg iron; 102mg sodium.

← Peaches & Cream Smoothie

If you make a lot of smoothies, keep peeled, quartered bananas in a tightly sealed container or bag in your freezer. Although this recipe doesn't call for the banana to be frozen, icy ones add an extra thickness and creaminess to smoothies.

MAKE IT

In a blender, mix together ½ cup vanilla or peach low-fat yogurt, 2 tablespoons low-fat milk, 2 tablespoons nonfat milk powder, ¼ cup frozen sliced peaches, and ¼ banana. Blend until smooth. Makes 1 smoothie.

Nutrition per smoothie: 189 calories; 11g protein; 2g fat (1g saturated fat); 33g carbohydrate; 1g fiber; 354mg calcium; 0mg iron; 141mg sodium.

HEY, YO!

Yogurt contains all the bone-building calcium of milk, plus stomach-soothing active cultures called probiotics. Look for a brand that is fortified with vitamin D; most kids (and parents) don't get enough of this nutrient.

← Top Pop

This recipe couldn't be any easier and you can just pull it out of the freezer whenever your kid is ready to eat.

MAKE IT

Push a Popsicle stick through the lid of a 4- to 6-ounce low-fat yogurt cup. Place in freezer until solid, a few hours (or overnight). Remove from freezer to soften a few minutes, wiggle out of carton, and serve. Makes 1 pop.

Nutrition per pop: 120 calories; 5g protein; 1g fat (1g saturated fat); 22g carbohydrate; 0g fiber; 172mg calcium; 0mg iron; 66mg sodium.

lunch

SOUPS • SALADS • SANDWICHES

Break out of the PB&J or mac 'n' cheese rut with this fresh batch of **kid-approved** midday meals. Many of them can be packed up **for school**, and all earn an "A" for nutrition.

Cheesy Broccoli & Potato Soup

You won't have any trouble getting your child to try something green when you put a bowlful of this creamy, potassium-packed soup on the table.

INGREDIENTS

- 2 teaspoons olive oil
- ½ onion, chopped
- 1 medium potato, peeled and diced into ½-inch pieces
- 3 cups chopped broccoli
- 3 cups low-sodium vegetable stock
- 1 cup shredded, reduced-fat Monterey Jack cheese

MAKE IT

1 In a large stockpot, heat oil and sauté the onion for 5 to 7 minutes over low to medium heat. Add potatoes, broccoli, and stock; bring to a boil. Reduce to a simmer and cook, covered, for 12 to 15 minutes or until broccoli and potatoes are tender when pierced with a fork.

2 Remove the mixture from stove top; allow to cool a bit. Pour the mixture and cheese into a blender; puree. (Puree it in batches if necessary.) Or use a handheld blender to do it right in the stockpot. Sprinkle a little extra cheese on top. Makes 4 cups.

Nutrition per cup: 170 calories; 13g protein; 9g fat (4g saturated fat); 13g carbohydrate; 3g fiber; 239mg calcium; 1mg iron; 377mg sodium.

kitchen tip

Here's another idea for getting kids to try broccoli: Roast it. Break it up into smallish florets, then toss with olive oil and a little salt and pepper. Spread in a single layer on a shallow baking pan and bake at 400°F for 15 to 20 minutes or until it's golden-brown on the tips and crispy.

Black Bean Soup

We snuck in sweet potatoes—their beta-carotene will give your child's immune system a boost. If you serve this soup in mugs, it will be easier for kids to enjoy.

INGREDIENTS

- 2 teaspoons vegetable oil
- 1 medium onion, chopped
- 1½ teaspoons cinnamon
- 2 cans (19 ounces each) no-salt-added black beans, with liquid
- 1 package (32 ounces) low-sodium chicken broth
- 1 large sweet potato, diced
  Plain Greek-style yogurt, optional

MAKE IT

1 In a saucepan, heat oil over medium heat. Add onion and cinnamon, and cook for 6 minutes. Stir in beans, chicken broth, and sweet potato. Bring mixture to a boil; reduce heat and simmer 10 minutes.

2 Let soup cool 5 minutes, puree in blender in two batches until smooth. Reheat on low until warm before serving. Divide among six mugs. Top with yogurt, if desired. Makes 6 servings.

Nutrition per serving: 201 calories; 13g protein; 2g fat (0g saturated fat); 34g carbohydrate; 10g fiber; 102mg calcium; 3mg iron; 137mg sodium.

nutrition note

Beans are a brilliant, budget-friendly source of protein and fiber—perfect for a child who doesn't like to eat red meat or chicken.

Asian Shrimp & Coconut Soup

With protein, veggies, and carbs, this soup is a well-balanced meal.

INGREDIENTS

- 1 tablespoon canola oil
- 1 tablespoon grated ginger
- 3 garlic cloves, minced
- 4 cups (32 ounces) low-sodium chicken broth
- 1 cup water
- 4 ounces angel-hair pasta, broken in half
- 1 cup snow peas, cut in half
- 1 cup matchstick carrots
- ½ cup coconut milk
- 1 pound precooked medium shrimp, cleaned and tails removed

MAKE IT

1 In a large saucepan, heat oil on medium-high. Cook ginger and garlic for 30 seconds. Pour in chicken broth and the water and bring to a boil over high heat. Add pasta and return to a boil. Cook for 3 minutes.

2 Toss in snow peas and matchstick carrots and cook another 3 minutes. Gently stir in coconut milk and shrimp and leave on the stove until shrimp is warmed through, about 2 to 3 minutes. Makes 8 cups.

Nutrition per cup: 190 calories; 16g protein; 6g fat (3g saturated fat); 14g carbohydrate; 1g fiber; 40mg calcium; 3mg iron; 216mg sodium.

nutrition note

To make this soup slightly lower in fat, you can substitute reduced-fat coconut milk for the regular stuff. Just be sure not to get cream of coconut, which is too sweet for this dish.

Ravioli & Meatball Soup

The teeny meatballs and cheese-filled pockets are the perfect size for toddlers and preschoolers.

INGREDIENTS

- ½ pound ground turkey breast
- 1 tablespoon Italian-seasoned bread crumbs
- ⅛ teaspoon ground sage
- ⅛ teaspoon pepper
- ⅛ teaspoon salt
- 3 cups low-sodium chicken broth
- 1 can (14.5 ounces) Italian-seasoned diced tomatoes
- 1 can (8 ounces) no-salt-added tomato sauce
- 1 cup chopped celery
- 1 cup chopped carrots
- 1 cup frozen green beans, thawed
- 1 package (7 ounces) refrigerated mini cheese ravioli, such as Buitoni

MAKE IT

1 Heat oven to 400°F. Line a baking pan with aluminum foil and coat with vegetable cooking spray. Combine turkey, bread crumbs, sage, pepper, and salt in a bowl; shape into 48 mini meatballs. Bake for 12 minutes, or until browned.

2 In a 3-quart saucepan, combine broth, tomatoes, tomato sauce, celery, and carrots. Boil, then reduce heat. Cover and simmer for 5 minutes. Cut up beans and stir into broth with ravioli. Cook, covered, for 5 minutes. Add meatballs to serve. Makes 8 cups.

Nutrition per 1¼ cups: 203 calories; 17g protein; 3g fat (1g saturated fat); 27g carbohydrate; 3g fiber; 89mg calcium; 2mg iron; 487mg sodium.

nutrition note

These mini meatballs are worth the effort. They're tasty and much lower in fat than store brands.

Watermelon Soup

If your kid doesn't like tomatoes, serve him watermelon more often. It contains many of the same nutrients, such as vitamin C and cancer-fighting lycopene.

INGREDIENTS

4½ cups watermelon cubes

½ teaspoon salt

¼ teaspoon ground coriander

⅛ teaspoon pepper

¼ cup plain Greek yogurt

2 tablespoons raisins

MAKE IT

1 Place the watermelon, salt, coriander, and pepper in a food processor or blender (split into two batches if equipment is small). Cover and puree until smooth. Mix in the Greek yogurt just until combined.

2 Serve soup in bowls and top with raisins to look like seeds. Makes about 3 cups.

Nutrition per ¾ cup: 76 calories; 3g protein; 1g fat (0 saturated fat); 17 carbohydrate; 1g fiber; 31mg calcium; 1mg iron; 298mg sodium.

kitchen tip

Greek yogurt is something of a miracle food—even the nonfat version adds richness and creaminess to dishes. In this recipe, it serves another purpose: It gives body to the soup so that the raisin "seeds" float on top.

Soup & Sandwich Combos

Keep your kids full and happy with these cute comfort-food pairs.

Strawberry Soup ➡

Vitamin C in the berries helps your child absorb the iron from the raisins and peanut butter.

MAKE IT

In a blender, combine 1 pint strawberries hulled and chopped; 1 cup low-fat vanilla yogurt; and 1 teaspoon lemon juice. Divide among four bowls and garnish each with a strawberry.

PB-and-Raisin Bagel ➡

Use regular or golden raisins for these sandwiches that are just the right size for little hands.

MAKE IT

Split 4 mini whole-wheat bagels and toast them. Thinly spread each half with 1 tablespoon peanut butter (use cream cheese for kids under 4) and top with ½ teaspoon raisins. Makes 4 servings.

Nutrition per combo (½ cup soup, 2 bagel halves): 405 calories; 18g protein; 18g fat (4g saturated fat); 51g carbohydrate; 8g fiber; 175mg calcium; 2mg iron; 399mg sodium.

Heart-y ➡ Pumpernickel

The creamy texture of hummus makes it a natural for kids. It works as a dip too.

MAKE IT

Place a heart-shaped cookie cutter over 1 slice of pumpernickel bread. Fill cutter with 2 tablespoons hummus, using a spoon or toothpick to push hummus to edge of form. Carefully pick up cutter to leave heart-shaped hummus. Repeat with 3 more slices of bread and 6 tablespoons hummus, divided. Makes 4 servings.

Carrot-Ginger Soup ➡

Celery and onions may seem like "nothing" foods, but they have a lot of healthy antioxidants. It's easy to slip them into this soup (or even pasta sauce) because they're pureed.

MAKE IT

Heat 1 tablespoon olive oil in a pot on medium-high. Add 1 small onion, chopped; 1 stalk celery, chopped; and 1 to 1½ tablespoons grated ginger. Sauté until soft, about 5 minutes. Add 1½ pounds sliced carrots and 2 cups low-sodium chicken broth. Bring to a boil and simmer until carrots are tender, about 25 minutes. Puree until smooth in a blender (let cool a bit first) or in the pot, using an immersion blender. Season to taste with salt and pepper. Divide among four bowls and garnish with chopped fresh chives.

Nutrition per combo (1 bowl of soup, 1 sandwich): 254 calories; 8g protein; 7g fat (1g saturated fat); 40g carbohydrate; 9g fiber; 101mg calcium; 2mg iron; 490mg sodium.

Beef & Bean Taco Salad

Ask your child to tear up the lettuce for the salad. She's more likely to eat the dish if she helps make it.

INGREDIENTS

- ¾ pound lean ground beef
- 1½ cups no-salt-added pinto or navy beans, drained
- ½ teaspoon chili powder
- ¼ teaspoon salt
- ⅛ teaspoon pepper
- ½ cup salsa, divided
- 1 tablespoon lime juice
- 1½ cups shredded lettuce
- ½ chopped avocado
- 1 small chopped tomato
- ¼ cup red-onion strips
- Baked tortilla strips

MAKE IT

1 In a large skillet, cook beef over medium heat. Drain well and return to pan. Mix in beans, chili powder, salt, and pepper; cook for 1 minute. Stir in ¼ cup salsa and heat through.

2 Mix together remaining salsa and lime juice; set aside. Divide lettuce among serving bowls. Add meat mixture, avocado, tomato, red onion, and salsa mixture. Finish by topping each salad with a handful of tortilla strips. Makes 4 servings.

Nutrition per serving: 329 calories; 23g protein; 12g fat (3g saturated fat); 31g carbohydrate; 7g fiber; 110mg calcium; 4mg iron; 355mg sodium.

cooking fun

Here are seven sous-chef tasks that preschoolers adore: Sprinkling cheese ✱ Dropping berries into batter ✱ Peeling bananas ✱ Cracking eggs (with help) ✱ Spray-coating a pan ✱ Mashing potatoes ✱ Snipping herbs (with kiddie scissors)

Greek Kabob Salad

If your kids complain about having lettuce on their plates, tell them that the kabobs need a "bed" to rest on.

INGREDIENTS

- 1 container (7 ounces) hummus
- ¼ cup lemon juice
- 2 tablespoons water
- 1 clove garlic, minced
- ¼ teaspoon salt
- ¼ teaspoon ground black pepper
- 1 pound pork tenderloin, cut into 1¼-inch cubes
- 2 teaspoons honey
- 1 red pepper, cut into bite-size chunks
- 1 package (8 ounces) mixed salad greens
- 1 medium cucumber, sliced

MAKE IT

1 Heat the broiler. In a small bowl, stir together the hummus, lemon juice, the water, garlic, salt, and pepper. Place the pork cubes in a large bowl. Top with half of the hummus mixture and stir together so it's mixed well. Add the honey to the remaining hummus mixture and set aside.

2 Alternately thread the pork and pepper pieces onto metal or wooden skewers (soak the wooden ones in water first), leaving ¼-inch space between pieces. Place skewers on the unheated rack of a broiler pan. Broil 4 inches from the heat for 12 to 15 minutes or until pork is done, turning every once in a while to brown evenly.

3 In a large bowl, combine the salad greens and cucumber. Toss with the reserved hummus mixture. Divide the vegetables among four serving plates. Place one kabob on top of each salad. Makes 4 servings.

Nutrition per serving: 263 calories; 27g protein; 8g fat (2g saturated fat); 21g carbohydrate; 4g fiber; 62mg calcium; 2mg iron; 329mg sodium.

kitchen tip

If your child likes to dip his veggies, try this salad dressing alternative. Make your own hummus by pureeing a can of drained chickpeas, 2 cloves pressed garlic, 1 to 2 tablespoons lemon juice, and 2 tablespoons tahini until smooth.

BLT in a Bowl

If your kids like the sandwich, give this equally delicious salad a shot. It's a great way to get them to start loving crunchy and nutritious greens.

INGREDIENTS

Salad

8 slices cooked low-sodium bacon, coarsely crumbled

4 cups sliced green-leaf lettuce

1 cup halved yellow and red grape tomatoes

1 cup croutons

Dressing

¼ cup light mayonnaise

1 tablespoon water

1 tablespoon cider vinegar

½ teaspoon sugar

Pinch of pepper

MAKE IT

1 Combine all the salad ingredients in a large bowl.

2 Whisk together the dressing ingredients in a small bowl. Drizzle the dressing over salad and toss it together. Makes 4 servings.

Nutrition per serving: 182 calories; 6g protein; 13g fat (4g saturated fat); 11g carbohydrate; 2g fiber; 29mg calcium; 1mg iron; 407mg sodium.

Shake-It-Up Salad

Strawberries, string cheese, and the fun of mixing it up help the lettuce go down. This meal packs a day's worth of vitamin C and then some.

INGREDIENTS

Salad

- 1 cup butter or Bibb lettuce
- ⅓ cup slivered carrots or your kid's favorite chopped vegetable
- 4 strawberries, sliced
- 1 stick reduced-fat swirled string cheese, sliced
- ¼ cup cubed low-sodium cooked ham

Dressing

- ½ cup low-fat buttermilk
- ½ cup light mayonnaise
- ½ tablespoon apple-cider vinegar
- 2 chives, chopped

MAKE IT

1 Cut or tear lettuce into small pieces. Toss together the lettuce, veggies, berries, cheese, and ham.

2 Pour the buttermilk, mayo, and vinegar into a medium bowl and whisk until combined. Gently stir in the chives. Transfer salad ingredients to bowl and serve dressing on the side. Store leftover dressing in the fridge. Makes 1 serving.

Nutrition per serving (with 2 tablespoons dressing): 186 calories; 12g protein; 11g fat (4g saturated fat); 12g carbohydrate; 3g fiber; 211mg calcium; 1mg iron; 517mg sodium.

nutrition note

Ranch or honey-mustard dressing? Cheddar cheese or mozzarella? When you let kids make some of the decisions about what goes into a salad—such as which vegetable goes into this one—they'll be more likely to give it a try.

Kiddie Cobb

Since the lettuce is on the bottom, kids won't even realize this is a salad until they start eating.

INGREDIENTS

2 cups chopped red-leaf lettuce

1 cup diced roast turkey, about ⅓ pound (use one thick slice from the deli)

1 ripe avocado, cut into chunks

½ cup halved red grapes

⅓ cup chickpeas

2 reduced-fat cheddar cheese sticks, cubed

Honey-mustard salad dressing

MAKE IT

Place lettuce on a serving platter. Line each of the remaining ingredients diagonally on top of lettuce, as shown, starting with turkey in the center. Serve with the dressing on the side. Makes 6 cups.

Nutrition per cup with 1 tablespoon dressing: 186 calories; 8g protein; 12g fat (3g saturated fat); 13g carbohydrate; 2g fiber; 91mg calcium; 1mg iron; 485mg sodium.

nutrition note

Protein-rich foods help build and repair every tissue in the body that kids need to grow. They also contain must-have nutrients—like iron, zinc, and B vitamins. Shop for the leanest meats (such as skinless chicken, turkey, or a cut of beef with "loin" or "round" in its name) to get protein minus the unhealthy fats. At least once a week, kids should eat fish and beans, which have nutrients that are not found in meat.

Mini Beef & Bulgur Burgers

When you use whole-grain bulgur in your hamburgers, you'll be able to cut back on ground beef, saving money and artery-clogging saturated fat.

INGREDIENTS

- 1 cup water
- ⅓ cup bulgur
- ¾ pound ground beef sirloin
- ½ cup finely chopped red onion
- ½ teaspoon salt
- ¼ teaspoon freshly ground black pepper
- 6 small whole-wheat buns or rolls, split and toasted
  Green or red lettuce leaves
- 1 tomato, sliced
- 1 avocado, halved, seeded, peeled, and sliced, optional

MAKE IT

1 Place the water in a medium saucepan and bring to boiling over high heat. Add the bulgur; cover, reduce heat, and simmer for 10 to 12 minutes or until tender. Remove from heat. Let stand, covered, for 5 minutes. Uncover; fluff with a fork. Cool.

2 In a large mixing bowl, combine the beef, onion, salt, pepper, and bulgur. Shape mixture into six ½-inch-thick patties.

3 Place the patties on the greased rack of an uncovered grill directly over medium coals. Grill for 10 to 12 minutes or until done, turning carefully once.

4 Serve burgers in buns topped with lettuce, tomato, and, if desired, avocado. Makes 6 servings.

Nutrition per serving: 265 calories; 16g protein; 12g fat (4g saturated fat); 25g carbohydrate; 6g fiber; 64mg calcium; 2mg iron; 372mg sodium

Sandwich Bouquets

If you're serving these super-cute sandwiches at a party or playdate, keep condiments on the side so they won't make the bread soggy.

INGREDIENTS

- 12 slices whole-wheat bread
- 12 slices white bread
- 2 tablespoons chocolate-hazelnut spread
- 2 tablespoons raspberry jam
- 3 slices low-sodium deli roast beef
- 6 thin cucumber slices
- 3 slices low-sodium ham
- 3 slices provolone cheese
- 3 slices low-sodium smoked turkey
- 3 slices reduced-fat Colby cheese

MAKE IT

1 Using the breads, make three of each kind of the following sandwiches: chocolate-hazelnut spread with raspberry jam; roast beef and cucumber slices; ham and provolone; and turkey with Colby.

2 With 1½- to 3-inch cookie cutters, cut the sandwiches into shapes. Cut center of top bread slices so filling shows through.

Nutrition range per sandwich: 156–240 calories; 6–15g protein; 3–9g fat (0–4g saturated fat); 23–36g carbohydrate; 2g fiber; 66–214mg calcium; 2mg iron; 298–581mg sodium.

kitchen tip

Save leftover bread from sandwich cut-outs and use it to make your own croutons or bread crumbs.

BBQ Pork Sandwiches

This quick and easy-to-prepare meal has half the fat of a cheeseburger—and tastes every bit as good.

INGREDIENTS

- 1 pound pork tenderloin, chopped
- 1 small onion, chopped
- 1 tablespoon vegetable oil
- 1 can (8 ounces) no-salt-added tomato sauce
- 3 tablespoons cider vinegar
- 1 tablespoon packed brown sugar
- 1 teaspoon yellow mustard
- 5 small rolls, split
- 2 cups coleslaw mix
- Sliced dill pickles

MAKE IT

1 Use a large skillet to brown the pork and onion in hot oil over medium heat for 2 to 3 minutes. Drain the fat and stir in the tomato sauce, vinegar, brown sugar, and mustard. Bring to a boil; reduce heat. Cover and simmer for 10 minutes, stirring occasionally. Uncover and cook for another 2 to 3 minutes, until the sauce reaches the consistency you like.

2 Spoon pork onto rolls and top with coleslaw mix and pickles. Makes 5 sandwiches.

Nutrition per sandwich: 343 calories; 25g protein; 8g fat (2g saturated fat); 40g carbohydrate; 3g fiber; 83mg calcium; 3mg iron; 526mg sodium.

kitchen tip

For a speedier version of this sandwich, substitute about 1¼ cups of your favorite bottled barbecue sauce for the tomato sauce, cider vinegar, brown sugar, and yellow mustard.

Plum-Good Chicken Burgers

Even with one-third the fat of a hamburger, these chicken patties remain moist thanks to the juicy plums on top. (And you thought we put them there just because they looked pretty!)

INGREDIENTS

- 1 pound ground chicken breast
- ¼ cup panko bread crumbs
- 1 tablespoon fresh basil, chopped
- ½ teaspoon ground ginger
- Salt and pepper to taste
- 1 plum
- 4 teaspoons olive oil, divided
- 6 square-shaped, 3-inch whole-grain buns, split
- 1 tablespoon sweet-and-sour sauce
- 12 baby spinach leaves

MAKE IT

1 In a bowl, combine chicken, bread crumbs, basil, ginger, salt, and pepper. Pat mixture into a 6-inch square on a piece of foil. Cover and freeze for 30 minutes so it gets firm. Meanwhile, halve the plum and remove the pit. Cut three ¼-inch-thick slices; make flower shapes with a cookie cutter. Don't discard the leftover pieces; they'll look cute on the burgers too and the plum's skin is particularly antioxidant-rich. Toss the plum slices with 1 teaspoon olive oil.

2 Cut chicken mixture into six 2⊠3-inch patties; brush with remaining oil. Grill on medium for 10 minutes or until done, turning once. Grill plums after you flip patties; turn once. Toast buns on grill rack for 1 minute.

3 Brush bottom of each bun with the sweet-and-sour sauce. Add 2 spinach leaves, chicken patty, plum cutout, and the bun top. Makes 6 burgers.

Nutrition per burger: 208 calories; 21g protein; 5g fat (1g saturated fat); 18g carbohydrate; 1g fiber; 51mg calcium; 2mg iron; 251mg sodium.

kitchen tip ● ● ● ●

Before grilling, brush meat or fish with olive oil, fruit juice, or an herb vinaigrette rather than BBQ sauce—it may help prevent carcinogens from forming on your food.

All-Star Sliders

Score a home run with these super-healthy sandwiches. Our sliders have half the fat of restaurant versions.

INGREDIENTS

- 2 skinless, boneless chicken breast halves
  Salt and pepper
  Vegetable cooking spray
- 4 slices white cheddar cheese
- 4 mini rolls
- 4 slices cucumber
- 4 baby spinach leaves
  Reduced-fat raspberry vinaigrette

MAKE IT

1 Using a mallet or a rolling pin, flatten chicken breast halves to about ¼- to ½-inch thick. Season both sides with salt and pepper and cut each in half crosswise so that you have four pieces.

2 Lightly coat a grill pan with cooking spray and heat on medium-high. Grill roll halves, cut sides down, for 1 to 2 minutes or until toasted; set aside. Add chicken and cook for 8 to 10 minutes, turning once. Remove chicken from pan and top with a cheese slice.

3 Meanwhile, use a cookie cutter to make star-shaped cucumbers. Secure the stars to tops of the rolls with a pick. Then place a piece of chicken and a spinach leaf inside of each roll. Pour vinaigrette into a dish so that your kids can spoon on their own dressing. Makes 4 servings.

Nutrition per serving: 273 calories; 23g protein; 10g fat; (4g saturated fat); 22g carbohydrate; 1g fiber; 154mg calcium; 2mg iron; 448mg sodium.

Junior Veggie Burgers

If your preschooler passed on the beans last night, don't worry. He won't even notice they're in this patty.

INGREDIENTS

- 2 tablespoons finely chopped carrot
- 2 tablespoons finely chopped red pepper
- 2 tablespoons frozen whole-kernel corn
- ½ cup cooked black beans
- ½ cup cooked brown rice
- 1 egg yolk
- 1 tablespoon fine dry bread crumbs
- 1 tablespoon olive oil
- 6 small whole-grain buns
- 6 small Bibb lettuce leaves
- 6 tomato slices
- ¼ cup plain yogurt
- 2 teaspoons honey mustard

MAKE IT

1 Place carrot, red pepper, and corn in a microwave-safe bowl and add 1 tablespoon water. Cover with wax paper and microwave on high for 2 minutes, or until tender. Drain and set aside.

2 Place beans and rice in a bowl and mash with a fork. Stir in cooked veggies and egg yolk. With wet hands, shape well-rounded tablespoons of mixture into balls, then roll in bread crumbs to coat. Flatten into 6 patties.

3 Heat oil in a skillet on medium. Cook patties for 2 to 3 minutes per side. Serve in buns with lettuce, tomato, and a dip made of stirred yogurt and honey mustard. Makes 6 servings.

Nutrition per serving: 183 calories; 7g protein; 6g fat (1g saturated fat); 27g carbohydrate; 4g fiber; 80mg calcium; 2mg iron; 177mg sodium.

Falafel Pockets

Crunchy falafel is a great burger alternative and packs a healthy protein punch.

INGREDIENTS

- 1   15-ounce can garbanzo beans
- ¼   cup shredded carrots
- 2   tablespoons all-purpose flour
- 3   tablespoons sesame tahini, divided
- 1½ teaspoons chopped garlic
- ½   teaspoon ground cumin
- ¼   teaspoon salt
- ⅛   teaspoon pepper
- 1   tablespoon olive oil or spray
- ⅓   cup plain low-fat yogurt
- 2   tablespoons lemon juice
- 1   tomato
- 4   lettuce leaves
- 8   mini whole-wheat pita pockets

MAKE IT

1 Heat oven to 425°F. Rinse and drain beans, and mash together with carrots, flour, 2 tablespoons tahini, 1 tablespoon water, garlic, cumin, salt, and pepper. It's fine if there are some pieces of garbanzos.

2 Grease a cookie sheet with olive oil and shape mixture into 16 patties the size of a half dollar. Place on cookie sheet. Brush with olive oil. Bake for 10 minutes or until crispy, turning once.

3 Meanwhile, in a small bowl mix yogurt, remaining tahini, and the lemon juice. Add warm water by the tablespoon if sauce seems stiff.

4 Stuff falafel, tomato, and lettuce leaves into pitas. Serve with yogurt sauce on the side and fresh veggies like cucumber and red-pepper dippers. Makes 4 servings.

Nutrition per serving: 415 calories; 16g protein; 65g carbohydrate, 12g fat (2g saturated fat), 11g fiber; 137mg calcium; 4mg iron; 354mg sodium.

kitchen tip

Falafel freezes beautifully either before or after cooking, so save leftovers or double the recipe.

CHAPTER 3

supper

MAIN DISHES • SIDE DISHES • PASTAS • ALL-IN-ONE DINNERS

Getting a **healthy dinner** on the table doesn't have to be stressful. With make-ahead meals, packaged shortcuts, and time-saving tricks, these **family recipes rock** so you can finally **relax** and enjoy your food.

Butterfly Shrimp Skewers

Shrimp is one of the best sources of selenium, a mineral that boosts the immune system. Serve these whimsical skewers with Citrusy Edamame (page 96) and brown rice.

INGREDIENTS

- 6 2-inch strips orange bell pepper
- 12 medium peeled and deveined uncooked shrimp
- 1 to 2 tablespoons reduced-fat vinaigrette salad dressing
- 12 cucumber slivers

MAKE IT

1 Soak six 8-inch wooden skewers in water for 30 minutes. Push a pepper strip into the center of each and cut two slits near the top. Place a shrimp on each side, as shown. Snip off the skewer's pointy ends if serving to young kids.

2 Brush shrimp and peppers with vinaigrette and grill on a greased rack over medium heat for 2 to 3 minutes or until shrimp are opaque, turning once. When cool enough to handle, add small strips of cucumber to slits for the butterfly's antennae. Makes 6 skewers.

Nutrition per skewer: 21 calories; 3g protein; 1g fat (0 saturated fat); 2g carbohydrate; 0g fiber; 8mg calcium; 0mg iron; 30mg sodium.

kitchen tip

If you forget to soak the skewers before grilling, wrap the exposed parts in aluminum foil to keep them from burning.

Tilapia Piccata

Pair these mild-tasting fillets glazed with a yummy lemon sauce with roasted Cauliflower "Popcorn" (page 96), and you've got a healthy fish dinner kids will ask for again and again.

INGREDIENTS

- ¼ cup all-purpose flour
- ½ teaspoon salt
- ¼ teaspoon pepper
- 1 pound (about 6) tilapia fillets
- 4 teaspoons canola oil
- 1 cup low-sodium chicken broth
- 1 teaspoon cornstarch
- 2 tablespoons lemon juice
- 1 tablespoon butter
- 1 tablespoon chopped parsley
- 2 tablespoons nonpareil capers, rinsed and drained, optional

MAKE IT

1 Combine flour, salt, and pepper in a shallow bowl. Dredge fish in flour mixture, coating well.

2 In a large nonstick skillet, heat oil on medium-high. Add fish and cook until brown, about 2 minutes. Flip and cook another minute. Transfer fish to a platter and keep warm.

3 Increase heat to high, add broth to skillet, and bring to a boil. Cook until liquid is reduced to ½ cup; it'll take about 3 minutes. Dissolve cornstarch in 1 tablespoon water; whisk into broth. Cook another minute, then stir in lemon juice, butter, parsley, and capers, if you're using them. Spoon the sauce over fish. Makes 6 servings.

Nutrition per serving: 99 calories; 7g protein; 5g fat (2g saturated fat); 5g carbohydrate; 0g fiber; 6mg calcium; 1mg iron; 249mg sodium.

cooking fun

Older kids can be a big help in the kitchen. Children ages 7 and up can gather ingredients and measure them out. But save the stove work for the teenagers.

Cod Cakes

These crisp, pan-fried patties are a great way to get your little landlubber to eat fish without a fuss. Serve them with a crunchy slaw, such as Rainbow Coleslaw (page 98).

INGREDIENTS

- 1 large potato, cut into 2-inch chunks
- ½ pound cod fillets
- 2 tablespoons grated Parmesan cheese
- 1 egg, lightly beaten
- 1 teaspoon chopped parsley
- 1 egg, lightly beaten
- 1 cup bread crumbs
- 2 tablespoons canola oil

Dip
- ¼ cup low-fat plain yogurt
- ¼ cup reduced-fat mayonnaise
- 1 tablespoon lemon juice
- ¼ teaspoon salt

MAKE IT

1 Place potato in a pot; add water to cover by 2 inches. Put on lid; cook 20 minutes on medium-high, or until tender. Lift out potatoes and mash in a bowl. Add cod fillets to the pot; cook 5 minutes and strain water. Gently break up cod. Add to potatoes in bowl, along with cheese, 1 egg, and parsley. Mix gently to combine.

2 Form mixture into 16 patties. Dip patties into another whisked egg and then into the bread crumbs. Heat 2 tablespoons canola oil in a large pan on medium. Cook cakes 4 minutes on each side, or until golden.

3 Stir together yogurt, mayonnaise, lemon juice, and the salt in a small bowl. Serve the dip on the side. Makes 16 2-inch patties and ½ cup dip.

Nutrition per 4 patties with 2 tablespoons sauce: 356 calories; 20g protein; 17g fat (3g saturated fat); 30g carbohydrate; 2g fiber; 133mg calcium; 2mg iron; 574mg sodium.

nutrition note

Many of the health benefits of seafood come from its omega-3 fatty acids, a type of polyunsaturated fat that is associated with heart health and brain function.

Fish & Veggies Baked in Parchment

This fish under wraps makes a super-easy and ultrahealthy one-dish meal.

INGREDIENTS

- 1 roll parchment paper
- 16 stalks asparagus, trimmed
- 8 small carrots, halved lengthwise
- 4 2.5-ounce tilapia fillets
- 1 tablespoon olive oil
- ½ teaspoon garlic-herb salt-free seasoning
- ⅛ teaspoon salt
- 4 thin orange slices, halved

MAKE IT

1 Heat oven to 400°F. Cut four 12-inch squares of parchment and fold in half. For each packet put 4 asparagus, 4 carrot halves, and 1 fillet on one side of the crease. Sprinkle with olive oil, seasoning, and salt.

2 Top with orange slices. Then, fold paper over fish and vegetables. Make two or three 1-inch folds on the short ends, then repeat on the long side to enclose. Arrange on a large baking sheet.

3 Bake for about 12 minutes. Check for doneness by unrolling a flap of paper (fish should flake easily and vegetables should be crisp-tender).

4 Using scissors, carefully cut through the top of each pack, pulling paper away to expose the fish and veggies. Makes 4 servings.

Nutrition per serving: 125 calories; 16g protein; 6g carbohydrate, 5g fat (1g saturated fat); 5g fiber; 2mg iron; 126mg sodium.

kitchen tip

Trim the asparagus by bending it near the woody end until it snaps.

Pecan-Crusted Fish Sticks

The crisp coating and buttery taste of pecans are a sure draw in this dish—and it's full of healthy fats too. Serve the fish sticks with Crinkly Carrot "Fries" (page 109) to create your own diner-style basket.

INGREDIENTS

Nonstick cooking spray

1 pound cod fillets, rinsed and patted dry

1 cup pecan halves

1 cup torn whole-wheat bread pieces

½ teaspoon salt

⅓ cup all-purpose flour

2 eggs, lightly beaten

MAKE IT

1 Heat oven to 450°F. Coat a wire baking rack with nonstick cooking spray and place on a baking sheet or in a shallow baking pan; set aside. Cut fish into fourteen 3×1-inch strips and set aside.

2 Place pecans, bread pieces, and salt in a food processor; pulse until fine. Place in small bowl. Put flour and eggs in separate bowls.

3 Lightly coat cod in flour. Dip in egg, and roll in pecan mixture. Put fish on rack; coat with cooking spray. Bake for 10 to 12 minutes or until golden. Makes 7, two-stick servings.

Nutrition per serving: 221 calories; 16g protein; 13g fat (2g saturated fat); 10g carbohydrate; 2g fiber; 32mg calcium; 1mg iron; 244mg sodium

nutrition note

All seafood contains at least a tiny bit of mercury, a toxic metal that interferes with the nervous system of fetuses and young children. Although a small amount occurs naturally, most of it enters the air and water supply when coal, wood, or oil are burned. Use Atlantic cod in this recipe—it's not overfished or high in mercury.

Citrus-Beef Kabobs

The orange marinade helps keep the lean beef moist and tender. Serve these kabobs with barley pilaf and French-style green beans. Stir half of the remaining orange juice mixture into the pilaf and toss the green beans with the other half to bump up the flavor of both sides.

INGREDIENTS

- 2 oranges
- 1 tablespoon olive oil
- 1 tablespoon reduced-sodium soy sauce
- 8 ounces beef sirloin, cut into strips

MAKE IT

1 Squeeze 3 tablespoons juice from one of the oranges and combine with oil and soy sauce. Add 1 tablespoon of the juice mixture to the beef; toss to coat.

2 Cut the other orange into 16 wedges. String two wedges and meat onto eight 8-inch skewers. (If using wooden skewers, soak in water for 30 minutes before using.) Cook in a grill pan over medium-high heat for 3 to 5 minutes or until meat is done, turning twice. Place kabobs on a platter to serve. Makes 4 two-kabob servings.

Nutrition per kabob: 64 calories; 7g protein; 3g fat (1g saturated fat); 3g carbohydrate; 0g fiber; 16mg calcium; 1mg iron; 89mg sodium.

Tandoori Chicken

This kid-friendly Indian dish introduces little ones to new flavor combos like garlic and ginger. Serve it with nutty-flavored brown rice and asparagus.

INGREDIENTS

- 1 pound chicken breast tenderloins
- 1 tablespoon vegetable oil
- 1 teaspoon garlic paste
- 1½ teaspoons garam masala
- 1 teaspoon grated fresh ginger

Dip
- 1 container (6 ounces) plain yogurt
- 1 tablespoon lime juice

MAKE IT

1 If using wooden skewers, soak in water for 30 minutes. Toss chicken with 1 tablespoon oil, garlic paste, garam masala, and ginger. Thread each piece onto a skewer.

2 Put the skewers right on the rack of a grill over medium heat (or cook on a grill pan) for about 10 minutes, turning occasionally. (Cook uncovered if you're using coals, but put the top down on a gas grill.)

3 For dip, mix yogurt and lime juice together and serve on the side. (Cut tips off skewers before serving to young kids.) Makes 8 skewers.

Nutrition per skewer: 109 calories; 15g protein; 5g fat (1g saturated fat); 2g carbohydrate; 0g fiber; 53mg calcium; 1mg iron; 67mg sodium.

kitchen tip

Garam masala, like curry powder, is a blend of spices used in Indian cooking. While the exact blend varies from brand to brand, it can include black pepper, cinnamon, cloves, coriander, cumin, cardamom, dried chilies, fennel, mace, nutmeg, and other spices. It's aromatic and adds a warmth to food but is not spicy.

Crispy Coconut Chicken

If you're in a hurry, you can cut the cooking time in half by using chicken breast strips instead of legs. Cooked peas tossed with brown rice makes a yummy accompaniment.

INGREDIENTS

- ⅔ cup crushed whole-grain crackers (about 8)
- ⅓ cup flaked coconut
- 1 jar (9 ounces) mango chutney
- 3 tablespoons lime juice
- 1 teaspoon curry powder
- 8 chicken drumsticks, skin removed

MAKE IT

1 Heat oven to 375°F. Place crackers in a large zip-top plastic bag and crush with a rolling pin. Add coconut to the bag and shake. In a small bowl, stir together the chutney, lime juice, and curry powder. Dip the chicken drumsticks, one piece at a time, in chutney, then place drumsticks inside the bag. Shake to coat.

2 Bake drumsticks on a foil-lined shallow baking pan for 40 minutes, or until cooked through (an instant-read thermometer inserted into the thickest part of the leg registers 180°F). Cover chicken loosely with aluminum foil for the last 10 minutes to prevent overbrowning. Makes 4 two-drumstick servings.

Nutrition per drumstick: 239 calories; 22g protein; 6g fat (2g saturated fat); 21g carbohydrate; 1g fiber; 14mg calcium; 1mg iron; 363mg sodium.

kitchen tip ●●●●

Most of the ingredients in this dinner are easily stored in the pantry or freezer. To help save money on the grocery bill, make a list of 10 to 20 nonperishable items that you buy regularly, and keep tabs on their prices at Parents.com's sister site, Recipe.com, for a few weeks so you'll know when you find a good deal. Stock up on these essentials when prices hit bottom.

Indian-Spiced Chicken with Relish

When the weather's nice, cook the chicken on your barbecue. Serve it with whole steamed green beans.

INGREDIENTS

- 2 pears, peeled, cored, and cut into chunks
- ½ cup fresh cranberries
- ⅓ cup dried cranberries
- 2 tablespoons honey
- 1 tablespoon cranberry or orange juice
- ½ teaspoon finely shredded orange peel
- ⅛ teaspoon ground ginger
- ½ teaspoon coarse kosher salt
- ½ teaspoon cumin
- ¼ teaspoon coarsely ground black pepper
- 4 skinless, boneless chicken-breast halves
- 1 tablespoon vegetable oil

  Vegetable cooking spray

MAKE IT

1 In a medium saucepan, combine the pears, fresh and dried cranberries, honey, and juice. Bring to a gentle boil and cook, uncovered, for 3 minutes. Remove from heat. Stir in orange peel and ginger. Set aside to cool slightly.

2 Meanwhile, stir together the salt, cumin, and pepper in a small bowl. Brush both sides of the chicken with oil and sprinkle with salt mixture. Lightly coat a grill pan with vegetable cooking spray; heat on medium-high. Add chicken to pan and cook for 12 minutes, or until cooked through (an instant-read thermometer inserted into the thickest part of the breast registers 170°F), turning once.

3 Slice the chicken and spoon the pear relish on the top. Makes 4 servings.

Nutrition per serving: 307 calories; 33g protein; 5g fat (1g saturated fat); 32g carbohydrate; 4g fiber; 30mg calcium; 1mg iron; 336mg sodium.

Moroccan Chicken

With just a few simple ingredients, you can enjoy this restaurant-style dish at home any day. Serve it with your favorite vegetable and/or grain as a side. We paired it with spinach, lentil, and tomato couscous.

INGREDIENTS

- 1 teaspoon ground cumin
- ½ teaspoon kosher salt
- ¼ teaspoon ground cinnamon
- 4 skinless, boneless chicken-breast halves
- 1 tablespoon vegetable oil

MAKE IT

1 Mix the cumin, salt, and cinnamon in a small bowl, and sprinkle them over the chicken. Heat the oil in a large skillet on medium. Add the chicken and cook about 8 to 12 minutes or until done, turning once.

2 Transfer the chicken from the skillet to a serving platter. Makes 4 servings.

Nutrition per serving: 189 calories; 33g protein; 5g fat (1g saturated fat); 0g carbohydrate; 0g fiber; 22mg calcium; 1mg iron; 334mg sodium.

kitchen tip

If you have paprika in your spice rack, sprinkle a bit on the chicken. It's often used in this classic North African dish.

Real Popcorn Chicken

This isn't like any popcorn chicken you've ever had—these tender chicken cutlets are covered in a crispy crust made from real popcorn! Seasoned with thyme and a squeeze of lemon juice, it's sure to become a family favorite. Serve it with Pinwheel Salad (page 102) or crunchy coleslaw.

INGREDIENTS

- 3 cups popped popcorn
- 1 tablespoon fresh thyme
- ¼ teaspoon salt
- ¼ teaspoon freshly ground black pepper
- 1 egg
- 3 tablespoons all-purpose flour
- 1 pound skinless, boneless chicken breast halves, cut into 2-inch pieces
- 1 tablespoon unsalted butter
- 1 tablespoon canola oil
- 1 lemon, cut into wedges

MAKE IT

1 Remove any unpopped popcorn kernels. Put the popcorn in a food processor; cover and pulse until coarsely ground. Place the popcorn in a shallow dish and add thyme, salt, and pepper.

2 Place the egg in another shallow dish; add 1 tablespoon water and beat lightly with a fork. Place flour in another shallow dish.

3 Dredge the chicken in the flour to coat, shaking off excess. Dip the chicken in the egg mixture, then in the popcorn mixture to coat.

4 Put the butter and oil in a large skillet over medium-high heat. Add chicken and cook 10 to 12 minutes or until chicken is cooked through, turning occasionally to brown evenly. Reduce to medium heat, if necessary. Serve with lemon wedges. Makes 4 servings.

Nutrition per serving: 249 calories; 30g protein; 9g fat (3g saturated fat); 12g carbohydrate; 2g fiber; 41mg calcium; 2mg iron; 239mg sodium.

Honey-Mustard Chicken Wings

These are as fun to eat as they are to make—serve them with lots of napkins and your favorite potato salad.

INGREDIENTS

3 pounds chicken wings, rinsed and patted dry with paper towels

2 tablespoons grapeseed or corn oil

Salt and freshly ground black pepper

¼ cup butter, melted

¼ cup Dijon mustard

2 tablespoons honey

Carrot sticks and celery sticks

MAKE IT

1 Heat oven to 375°F. Put the chicken wings in a large roasting pan, drizzle with the oil, and sprinkle liberally with salt and pepper. Toss to coat and spread the wings out in a single layer.

2 Roast, undisturbed, until the bottom of the pan is coated with fat and the wings are beginning to brown, about 15 minutes. Use a spoon to baste the wings with the drippings, then carefully pour the extra fat out of the pan and flip them over (if they're sticking, give them an extra 5 minutes).

3 Combine melted butter with Dijon mustard and honey. Toss the wings with the butter mixture.

4 Return wings to the oven until both sides are nicely browned, another 10 minutes or so (they'll release easily from the pan when ready).

5 Raise the oven temperature to 450°F and continue to cook until wings are crisp all over, about 10 more minutes. Serve hot, warm, or at room temperature with carrot and celery sticks on the side. Makes 6 to 8 servings.

Nutrition per serving: 309 calories; 17g protein; 24g total fat (8 g saturated fat); 4g carbohydrate; 0g dietary fiber; 13mg calcium; 1mg iron; 371mg sodium.

Pulled Pork & Pepper Wraps

Try serving these with wedges of ripe cantaloupe or low-fat, low-sodium refried beans.

INGREDIENTS

- 1 pound pork tenderloin
  Salt and pepper
- ½ cup barbecue sauce
- ¼ cup apricot spreadable fruit or low-sugar apricot jam
- ⅓ cup chopped onion
- ½ cup strips assorted-color sweet peppers
- 6 whole-wheat tortillas
  Assorted toppings (shredded cheddar cheese, salsa, guacamole, and/or light sour cream)

MAKE IT

1 Season pork with salt and pepper. Place pork in a 4-quart slow cooker. In a bowl, mix barbecue sauce, spreadable fruit, and onion; pour over pork. Add peppers. Cover; cook on low-heat setting for 4 hours or on high-heat setting for 2 hours. The pork should be at least 160°F.

2 Remove pork and cut up; shred with fork. Stir back into mixture in cooker. Serve in flour tortillas with the assorted toppings. Makes 6 wraps.

Nutrition per wrap (without toppings): 291 calories; 20g protein; 5g fat (1g saturated fat); 39g carbohydrate; 2g fiber; 108mg calcium; 2mg iron; 460mg sodium.

Cranberry Pork Chops

The sweetness of the cranberry-orange sauce makes kids love this dish. It's delicious served with a cooked whole-grain blend, such as brown rice with pecans and garlic.

INGREDIENTS

- 1 tablespoon vegetable oil
- 1 medium yellow onion, halved and sliced
- 4 boneless pork-loin chops, cut 1 inch thick
  Salt and pepper
- 1 can (16 ounces) whole cranberry sauce
- ¼ cup orange juice

MAKE IT

1 In a large skillet, heat oil over medium-high heat. Add onion and cook until tender, about 4 minutes. Season pork chops with salt and pepper and add to skillet. Cook until browned on both sides, about 4 minutes. Leave chops in pan.

2 Add cranberry sauce and orange juice to skillet and stir. Heat just to a boil. Reduce heat to low and simmer, covered, 5 to 7 minutes more. Top with the fruit sauce. Makes 4 servings.

Nutrition per serving: 486 calories; 20g protein; 17g fat (5g saturated fat); 48g carbohydrate; 2g fiber; 14mg calcium; 1mg iron; 205mg sodium.

A New Spin On Veggies

Kids gravitate toward certain vegetables—but they'll be open to more adventurous options if they're cooked in a special way.

Cauliflower "Popcorn" ⬆

Roasted cauliflower has a nutty flavor.

MAKE IT

Toss 3 cups small cauliflower florets with 2 tablespoons olive oil and ¼ teaspoon pepper. Roast at 450°F, uncovered, for 20 minutes or until lightly browned, stirring once or twice. Sprinkle with 2 tablespoons grated Parmesan cheese.

Nutrition per ½ cup: 60 calories; 2g protein; 5g fat (1g saturated fat); 3g carbohydrate; 1g fiber; 30mg calcium; 0mg iron; 41mg sodium.

⬅ Citrusy Edamame

These super-healthful green soybeans make a delicious snack too.

MAKE IT

Cook 2 cups fresh or frozen shelled edamame according to the package directions; drain. Toss with 1 tablespoon olive oil, ½ teaspoon finely shredded orange peel, ¼ teaspoon dried dill weed, and ¼ teaspoon salt.

Nutrition per ½ cup: 150 calories; 10g protein; 8g fat (1g saturated fat); 9g carbohydrate; 4g fiber; 102mg calcium; 2mg iron; 156mg sodium.

Greek Stuffed Mushrooms →

A yummy filling in an edible bowl!

MAKE IT

Bake 12 mushroom caps, with the smooth side up, at 425°F for 5 minutes. Sauté ½ cup chopped mushroom stems along with 1 clove minced garlic in hot olive oil on medium heat until tender. Remove from stove; stir in ¼ cup seasoned bread crumbs, 1 chopped fresh plum tomato, 1 tablespoon pine nuts, and ¼ cup crumbled feta cheese. Fill caps with mixture and bake for 8 to 10 minutes more.

Nutrition per mushroom: 39 calories; 1g protein; 2g fat (1g saturated fat); 3g carbohydrate; 1g fiber; 24mg calcium; 0mg iron; 80mg sodium.

← Bacon Brussels Sprouts

When cooked properly, Brussels sprouts are absolutely delicious. A little bacon doesn't hurt, either.

MAKE IT

Boil 12 ounces Brussels sprouts, trimmed and halved, in lightly salted water for 5 minutes. Meanwhile, sauté 2 slices turkey bacon in 1 tablespoon canola oil on medium-high heat. Remove the bacon and crumble. Add cooked Brussels sprouts to the skillet; cook 2 minutes. Stir in bacon, salt, and pepper until heated. Drizzle with 1 tablespoon red-wine vinegar before serving. Makes 4 cups.

Nutrition per ¾ cup: 54 calories; 2g protein; 3g fat (1g saturated fat); 5g carbohydrate; 2g fiber; 22mg calcium; 1mg iron; 170mg sodium.

Rainbow Coleslaw

There's no rule that coleslaw has to be cabbage slathered in creamy, high-fat dressing—and this fresh-tasting slaw made with summer squash is proof positive.

INGREDIENTS

- 2 yellow summer squash
- 1 large carrot
- 1 medium red apple
- 2 tablespoons olive oil
- 2 tablespoons cider vinegar
- 1½ teaspoons fresh dill
  Salt and pepper to taste

MAKE IT

Use a vegetable peeler to cut strips from squash and carrot. Place in a large bowl. Cut 4 slices from the apple; peel long, thin strips from each slice. Add to bowl. Whisk oil, vinegar, dill, salt, and pepper and toss into the slaw. Serve, or cover and chill for up to 24 hours. Makes 3 cups.

Nutrition per ½ cup: 71 calories; 1g protein; 5g fat (1g saturated fat); 7g carbohydrate; 2g fiber; 20mg calcium; 0 iron; 112mg sodium.

kitchen tip

You can use any type of apple in this coleslaw recipe, but the Red Delicious variety tastes best in this case because it's super sweet.

Spinach & Pear Salad

Put the kids' dressing on the side, so they can switch to another flavor if they don't like the vinaigrette.

INGREDIENTS

- 2 pears, cored and each cut into 8 equal-size wedges
- 2 tablespoons olive oil, divided
- 2 cups cubed whole-wheat French or Italian bread
- 1 clove garlic, minced
- ¼ teaspoon salt
- ⅛ teaspoon ground black pepper
- ¼ cup walnut pieces (for kids 4 and older)
- 4 cups fresh baby spinach leaves
- ⅓ cup pre-crumbled goat cheese
- ¼ cup red wine or balsamic vinaigrette

MAKE IT

1 Heat oven to 425°F. Toss pear wedges with 1 tablespoon olive oil and arrange them in a single layer in one half of a baking pan. In a medium bowl, mix together the bread cubes, garlic, salt, pepper, and the remaining olive oil. Spread the mixture flat in the other half of the baking pan and top with nuts.

2 Bake for 8 minutes, or until pears are tender and bread and nuts are toasted. Place pan on a wire rack to cool.

3 Divide spinach among four plates. Top with pears, bread-nut mixture, goat cheese, and vinaigrette. Makes 4 servings.

Nutrition per serving: 329 calories; 23g protein; 12g fat (3g saturated fat); 31g carbohydrate; 7g fiber; 110mg calcium; 4mg iron; 355mg sodium.

nutrition note

Ideally, you'll divide daily fruit and vegetable servings fairly equally between the two. But if you have a picky eater, set this minimum goal: Have at least one serving of dark-green or orange veggies every day. They have unique disease-preventing compounds. And take comfort in the fact that tomato sauce or soup, salsa, and baked fries count toward your child's vegetable servings too.

Pinwheel Salad

Cool shapes, fun toppings, and colorful dressings will win over your picky eater. It's a breeze to make this salad, especially if you use precut veggies.

INGREDIENTS

2 hearts of romaine

1 seedless cucumber, sliced

1 cup sweet red pepper slices

¾ cup sliced crinkle-cut carrots

¾ cup halved cherry tomatoes

½ cup sliced celery

Caesar or ranch dressing

MAKE IT

Placing romaine first, on four serving plates arrange ingredients to form a pinwheel, as shown. Give each person a small cup of dressing to use as a dip. Makes 4 servings.

Nutrition per salad with 2 tablespoons dressing: 201 calories; 2g protein; 17g fat (3g saturated fat); 10g carbohydrate; 3g fiber; 46mg calcium; 1mg iron; 386mg sodium.

nutrition note

Heads up: It's a long shot that kids will eat spring mix or any of the more bitter varieties of lettuce. Butterhead, romaine, and iceberg are better picks, and still supply plenty of nutrients.

Orange Crush

Your kid will be wooed by the chow mein noodles; they're even more fun than croutons.

INGREDIENTS

- ½ head iceberg lettuce, sliced
- 2 cups baby spinach leaves
- 1 can (6.1 ounces) mandarin orange segments, drained
- ½ cup chow mein noodles
   Asian-ginger salad dressing

MAKE IT

Toss lettuce and spinach together in a serving bowl. Arrange orange segments in a circle on top. Place noodles, crushed or whole, in the center of oranges. Serve dressing on the side. Makes 4 salads.

Nutrition per salad (without dressing): 125 calories; 2g protein; 6g fat (1g saturated fat); 15g carbohydrate; 2g fiber; 46mg calcium; 2mg iron; 236mg sodium.

Caprese Bread Salad

It's a traditional caprese salad with grilled whole-grain croutons for a kid-friendly touch. Try serving it with simple roasted or grilled chicken.

INGREDIENTS

- 4 ½-inch-thick slices whole-grain bread (about 6 ounces total)
- 1 cup grape tomatoes
- 6 ounces part-skim mozzarella cheese or fresh mozzarella cheese, cut into cubes
- 3 tablespoons chopped fresh basil
- 2 tablespoons olive oil
- 1 tablespoon balsamic vinegar
- ⅛ teaspoon black pepper

MAKE IT

1 Place bread slices on the rack of a charcoal grill over medium-hot coals. Place tomatoes in a disposable foil pan. Place on grill next to bread. Cover and grill for 1 to 2 minutes or until bread is toasted and tomatoes are charred, turning bread once and shaking pan with tomatoes occasionally. (For a gas grill, preheat grill. Reduce heat to medium-high. Add bread and tomatoes to grill rack. Grill as above.)

2 Cut bread into ½-inch cubes. Slice tomatoes in half. In a large bowl, combine bread, tomatoes, cheese, basil, oil, vinegar, and pepper; toss to coat. Makes 4 servings.

Nutrition per serving: 286 calories; 17g protein; 15g fat (5g saturated fat); 21g carbohydrate; 5g fiber; 374mg calcium; 2mg iron; 397mg sodium.

Making Familiar Veggies Fun

Put something in front of your picky eater that looks familiar but has just a bit of a twist. This simple strategy will get him to start trying (and yes, loving) his veggies.

Sunny Broccoli ↑

It's pretty to look at and tasty to eat.

MAKE IT

Steam 3 cups broccoli florets for 5 minutes. Toss with 2 tablespoons orange juice, 1 tablespoon canola oil, 1 clove minced garlic, salt, and pepper. Spoon mixture onto small orange slices arranged in the shape of a flower. Makes 6 servings.

Nutrition per ½ cup broccoli and ½ orange: 51 calories; 1g protein; 2g fat (0g saturated fat); 7g carbohydrate; 1g fiber; 30mg calcium; 0mg iron; 108mg sodium.

← Minty Peas

Of all of the green vegetables, sweet-tasting peas are one of the easiest to get kids to try.

MAKE IT

Sauté 2 cups peas in 2 teaspoons olive oil on medium for 2 minutes. Remove from heat; add 2 tablespoons fresh mint, 1 teaspoon lemon zest, and a dash of salt and pepper. Makes 4 servings.

Nutrition per ½ cup: 77 calories; 4g protein; 2g fat (0g saturated fat); 10g carbohydrate; 3g fiber; 22mg calcium; 1mg iron; 115mg sodium.

Cucumber Ribbon Salad ➡

Tossed with a slightly sweet sesame dressing, these crisp cukes will disappear in a flash.

MAKE IT

Trim the ends off a medium cucumber, then cut it in half crosswise and peel into strips. Whisk 2 tablespoons rice vinegar, 1 tablespoon canola oil, ½ teaspoon toasted sesame oil, ½ teaspoon honey, salt, and pepper. Toss the dressing with the cucumber and some toasted sesame seeds. Makes 4 servings.

Nutrition per serving: 68 calories; 1g protein; 5g fat (1g saturated fat); 5g carbohydrate; 1g fiber; 16mg calcium; 1mg iron; 148mg sodium.

⬅ Crinkly Carrot "Fries"

They may look like the potatoes you get at your favorite diner, but these are packed with vitamins A and C—and they come without the greasiness of the deep-fried variety.

MAKE IT

Slice 1 pound carrots into ½-inch-wide sticks using a crinkle cutter. Toss with 1 tablespoon olive oil, ½ teaspoon dried thyme, and ¼ teaspoon salt. Bake at 400°F for 15 to 20 minutes, or until soft. Makes 4 servings.

Nutrition per serving: 48 calories; 1g protein; 2g fat (0g saturated fat); 6g carbohydrate; 2g fiber; 23mg calcium; 0mg iron; 144mg sodium.

Healthy Fried Rice

Your kid might actually eat his veggies if they're in this Chinese fave. Feel free to replace the frozen mixed vegetables with fresh ones.

INGREDIENTS

- 4 teaspoons canola oil, divided
- 3 eggs
- 1 16-ounce package mixed frozen vegetables
- 1 cup frozen peppers-and-onion stir-fry vegetables
- 3 tablespoons stir-fry sauce
- ½ teaspoon crushed red pepper (optional)
- 1 8.8-ounce package cooked brown rice
- Lime wedges

MAKE IT

1 Heat 2 teaspoons canola oil in a large nonstick skillet on medium. Whisk eggs and add to the skillet. Cook, stirring occasionally to break up eggs, until set. Remove from pan. Add remaining 2 teaspoons oil to the skillet and then increase the heat to medium-high. Stir in the frozen vegetables; cook for 5 minutes or until tender.

2 Add stir-fry sauce and crushed red pepper, if using, to the skillet. Stir in rice and heat through, then mix in the cooked eggs. Let your kids squeeze on lime juice to give the dish extra flavor. Makes 4 servings.

Nutrition per serving: 252 calories; 9g protein; 10g fat (2g saturated fat); 30g carbohydrate; 2g fiber; 30mg calcium; 1mg iron; 483mg sodium.

nutrition note

This dish cuts the calories and sodium of a typical takeout version by nearly half—plus it's made with whole-grain rice.

Farotto with Peas & Parmesan

Take the fabulous flavor of farro—rich and earthy—and treat it like risotto. Then add sweet peas and Parmesan and you've got the perfect side dish, a starch and a vegetable all in one!

INGREDIENTS

- 1 tablespoon olive oil
- ⅓ cup chopped onion
- 1 cup farro (spelt)
- 4 cups no-salt-added chicken broth, warmed in a saucepan
- 1 tablespoon unsalted butter
- 1 cup finely shredded Parmesan cheese
- 1 cup frozen peas

MAKE IT

1 Put the oil in a large saucepan over medium heat. Add the onion; cook and stir for 5 minutes or until tender. Add the farro and cook and stir for 2 minutes or until toasted.

2 Using a ladle or measuring cup, begin adding broth to the farro, about ½ cup at a time. Cook and stir after each addition until liquid is absorbed. Continue adding broth, stirring frequently, until the farro is tender but not mushy (about 40 minutes).

3 Stir in the butter, Parmesan, and peas. Cook and stir to heat through. Serve immediately. Makes 6 servings.

Nutrition per serving: 243 calories; 13g protein; 9g fat (4g saturated fat); 28g carbohydrate; 5g fiber; 175mg calcium; 2mg iron; 353mg sodium.

nutrition note

At least half of your kids' grain servings should be the unrefined type—like whole wheat, farro, or oats—because they pack more vitamin E, magnesium, and fiber than their processed counterparts. These whole grains may also reduce your kids' risk of asthma, diabetes, and, later in life, heart disease.

Corn & Edamame Salad

Since many kids already like corn, we put it in this dish with other veggies they may be reluctant to try solo.

INGREDIENTS

- 3 ears corn on the cob
- 2 tablespoons plus 1 teaspoon olive oil, divided
- 1½ cups frozen shelled edamame, cooked and drained
- 1 tomato, seeded and chopped
- ½ slivered green sweet pepper, or your favorite color
- 2 tablespoons red-wine vinegar
- 1 clove garlic, minced
- Salt and pepper to taste

MAKE IT

1 Husk corn and brush with 1 teaspoon oil. Grill on medium heat about 15 minutes, or until tender, turning occasionally to brown evenly. Remove and let cool.

2 Cut kernels from the corncobs into a large bowl. Add edamame, chopped tomato, and sweet pepper. In a small bowl, whisk together the remaining oil, vinegar, garlic, salt, and pepper. Stir dressing into corn mixture. Serve at room temperature or cover and chill for up to 3 days. Makes about 6 cups.

Nutrition per cup: 127 calories; 5g protein; 7g fat (1g saturated fat); 13g carbohydrate; 3g fiber; 23mg calcium; 1mg iron; 59mg sodium.

kitchen tip

If your family eats a lot of fresh corn, add a corn stripper to your kitchen tool kit. This gadget removes several rows with one stroke of your hand. It's widely available at kitchen stores and online.

Feeling Saucy?

If your kid dislikes the taste of plain veggies, flavor them with a sauce he does enjoy, such as honey-mustard or teriyaki.

Cheesy ↑ Spaghetti Squash

MAKE IT

Place half of a 2½-pound seeded spaghetti squash, cut side down, in a baking dish with 2 tablespoons water; cover with wax paper. Microwave on high for 10 to 12 minutes, or until tender. Let cool slightly, then scrape strands from squash. Toss with 1 cup pasta sauce and 3 tablespoons shredded Parmesan cheese. Makes 4 to 6 servings.

Nutrition per 1 cup: 48 calories; 2g protein; 1g fat (0g saturated fat); 8g carbohydrate; 1g fiber; 54mg calcium; 1mg iron; 215mg sodium.

← Honey-Glazed Carrots

MAKE IT

Boil ½ pound peeled baby carrots in lightly salted water for 5 minutes; drain. In same pan, melt 1 tablespoon butter on medium; stir in 1 tablespoon honey and ½ teaspoon ground ginger. Boil 1 minute while stirring. Fold in carrots and 1 tablespoon chopped parsley. Makes 4 servings.

Nutrition per ¾ cup: 62 calories; 1g protein; 3g fat (2g saturated fat); 9g carbohydrate; 2g fiber; 21mg calcium; 1mg iron; 65mg sodium.

Teriyaki Green Beans ➡

A little bit of sweetness from the teriyaki sauce and the crunch of toasted almonds makes these green beans irresistible.

MAKE IT

Cook 3 cups (24 ounces) frozen whole green beans according to package directions. Drain and toss with 2 tablespoons minced shallots, 2 tablespoons light teriyaki sauce, and ¼ cup toasted slivered almonds. Makes 6 servings.

Nutrition per ½ cup: 58 calories; 2g protein; 2g fat (0g saturated fat); 7g carbohydrate; 2g fiber; 39mg calcium; 1mg iron; 146mg sodium.

⬅ Breaded Asparagus

You can give your child a small condiment cup of the honey-mustard sauce. Double-dipping is OK—even encouraged!

MAKE IT

Dip 8 ounces trimmed asparagus spears first in all-purpose flour, then in beaten egg, and then in panko bread crumbs. Drizzle asparagus with 1 tablespoon olive oil. Bake in a single layer at 450°F for 10 minutes, or until golden. Serve with honey-mustard dip. Makes 4 servings.

Nutrition per 6 pieces: 146 calories; 4g protein; 8g fat (1g saturated fat); 14g carbohydrate; 2g fiber; 23mg calcium; 2mg iron; 249mg sodium.

Healthy Carbonara

The classic Italian recipe calls for heavy cream, but you'll save about 75 calories and 11g fat per serving by making this version with fat-free half-and-half.

INGREDIENTS

- 1 (9-ounce) package fettuccine
- 1 cup frozen green peas
- 3 slices center-cut bacon
- 1 small onion, chopped
- 3 garlic cloves, minced
- ½ teaspoon dried thyme
- ½ cup fat-free half-and-half
- ½ cup shredded Parmesan

MAKE IT

1 Cook pasta according to the directions on the package, but don't salt the water. Three minutes before the pasta is supposed to be done, add the green peas to the pot. Drain, and reserve ¾ cup of cooking liquid.

2 Meanwhile, cook bacon in a large saucepan on medium-high until crispy. Remove bacon from pan and discard all except 2 teaspoons of drippings. Add onion to the pan and sauté for 3 minutes in the leftover drippings. Add garlic and thyme, and cook another minute. Stir in pasta and peas, reserved cooking liquid, and half-and-half. Cook 2 minutes. Crumble bacon on top of pasta and toss with cheese. Makes 4 servings.

Nutrition per serving: 364 calories; 16g protein; 6g fat (3g saturated fat); 60g carbohydrate; 4g fiber; 194mg calcium; 3mg iron; 362mg sodium.

nutrition note

Center-cut bacon has about 20 percent less saturated fat than regular bacon because it is cut closer to the bone.

Butternut Squash Casserole

This dish helps kids warm up to butternut squash—and delivers a lot of calcium in the form of toasty, gooey low-fat white cheddar.

INGREDIENTS

- ½ butternut squash, peeled and cut into ½-inch cubes (2 cups)
- 2 teaspoons olive oil
- ¼ teaspoon salt
- ½ pound whole-wheat elbows
- 2 tablespoons butter
- 2 tablespoons flour
- 1½ cups reduced-fat milk
- 1¾ cups low-fat white cheddar cheese, shredded and divided

MAKE IT

1 Heat oven to 375°F. Toss squash with oil and salt on a foil-lined tray. Bake for 20 minutes or until tender; set aside.

2 Cook pasta for 2 minutes less than package directions call for; drain and place in a bowl with squash. Meanwhile, melt butter over low heat. Whisk in flour; cook for 2 minutes.

3 Slowly whisk in milk. Bring mixture to a boil, then simmer. Cook 3 minutes, stirring occasionally. Add 1½ cups cheese; stir until melted. Stir cheese sauce into pasta and squash.

4 Spoon into 6 greased individual ramekins. Sprinkle on remaining cheese. Bake 10 minutes. Makes 6 servings.

Nutrition per serving: 330 calories; 17g protein; 13g fat (7g saturated fat); 39g carbohydrate; 3g fiber; 329mg calcium; 2mg iron; 349mg sodium.

nutrition note

Lower-fat cheeses are packed with just as much calcium (and sometimes more!) than their heftier counterparts. An ounce of reduced-fat mozzarella, cheddar, Colby, Muenster, provolone, and Swiss, or ½ cup of part-skim ricotta, supplies at least 25 percent of the calcium that 4- to 8-year-olds need daily for strong bones and teeth.

Low-Maintenance Lasagna

No need to boil noodles or align them perfectly in a pan! This slow-cooker version of the family fave requires just 10 minutes of hassle-free prep.

INGREDIENTS

Nonstick cooking spray

1 26-ounce jar pasta sauce

¾ cup water

1 15-ounce carton part-skim ricotta cheese

½ cup shredded carrots

6 regular lasagna noodles

1½ cups part-skim shredded mozzarella cheese (6 ounces)

MAKE IT

1 Coat a 4-quart slow cooker with cooking spray. In a large microwave-safe bowl, stir together the pasta sauce and the water. Cover with wax paper and microwave on high for about 3 minutes. In the meantime, in a medium bowl, stir together ricotta cheese and carrots; set aside.

2 Spoon ½ cup of the sauce mixture in the bottom of the slow cooker. Break half of the noodles and arrange over the sauce. Spoon half of the ricotta mixture over the noodles. Continue layering in the following order: ½ cup mozzarella, half of the remaining sauce, remaining noodles (breaking them to fit), the remaining ricotta mixture, ½ cup mozzarella, the rest of the sauce, and the rest of the mozzarella.

3 Cover; cook on low-heat setting for about 3 hours, until the noodles are tender. Remove liner from slow cooker; let cool, covered, for about 20 minutes so lasagna will be easier to slice. Makes 6 servings.

Nutrition per serving: 286 calories; 18g protein; 10g fat (5g saturated fat); 31g carbohydrate; 3g fiber; 397mg calcium; 1mg iron; 646mg sodium.

Pumpkin Penne

Thanks to canned pumpkin, this pasta dish gives the kiddos two servings of veggies. This meatless meal also has as much iron as a burger.

INGREDIENTS

- 1 12-ounce box whole-wheat penne
- 1 tablespoon olive oil
- 1 shallot, finely chopped
- 1½ cups low-sodium chicken broth
- ½ cup fat-free evaporated milk
- 1 15-ounce can pumpkin
- ½ teaspoon pumpkin-pie spice
- ¼ teaspoon salt
- ¼ teaspoon pepper
- Fresh parsley, chopped
- 1½ ounces Parmesan cheese, grated

MAKE IT

1 Cook pasta according to package directions. Drain and return to pot, covering to keep warm.

2 Meanwhile, in a saucepan, heat oil on medium. Add shallot; cook and stir until tender, about 3 minutes. Whisk in broth, evaporated milk, pumpkin, spice, salt, and pepper. Bring to a boil; reduce heat to low. Simmer, uncovered, for 4 minutes, stirring occasionally.

3 Toss pasta with sauce. Spoon into bowls and top with parsley and cheese. Makes 6 cups.

Nutrition per cup: 308 calories; 13g protein; 6g fat (2g saturated fat); 51g carbohydrate; 2g fiber; 188mg calcium; 3mg iron; 287mg sodium.

nutrition note

Pumpkin is packed with vitamin A in the form of the powerful antioxidant beta-carotene. At breakfast, add a couple tablespoons of canned pumpkin to your next batch of pancakes.

Nutty Noodles

Pasta with PB? Kids will slurp it up—veggies and all.

INGREDIENTS

- 8 ounces buckwheat (soba) noodles or whole-wheat thin spaghetti
- 1 cup crinkle-cut carrots
- 2 cups frozen shelled edamame
- 1 cup snow peas, trimmed and halved lengthwise
- ½ cup Thai peanut sauce
- 2 tablespoons creamy peanut butter
- 2 tablespoons reduced-sodium soy sauce
- Chopped fresh cilantro
- Coarsely chopped dry-roasted peanuts (for kids age 4 and over)

MAKE IT

1 Bring lightly salted water to a boil in a large saucepan. Add noodles and carrots, return to boiling and cook 5 minutes. Stir in edamame and snow peas; cook, uncovered, for 3 to 5 minutes longer or until noodles and vegetables are tender. Drain and return to saucepan.

2 In a medium bowl, mix together peanut sauce, peanut butter, and soy sauce until it's smooth. Stir the peanut sauce into pan with the noodles and veggies. Sprinkle on the cilantro and peanuts. Makes 6 servings.

Nutrition per serving: 342 calories; 16g protein; 12g fat (4g saturated fat); 46g carbohydrate; 7g fiber; 104mg calcium; 3mg iron; 596mg sodium.

nutrition note

Soba noodles are a Japanese buckwheat pasta that boasts fiber, manganese, and magnesium. It has half the calories of spaghetti.

Cheesy Linguine with Clams

If your kid doesn't dig clams, no worries. This pasta tastes just like noodles and butter—the clams are shelled and blend right in!

INGREDIENTS

- ½ pound dried linguine
- 3 tablespoons olive oil
- 2 cloves garlic, minced
- 2 dozen shucked clams, finely chopped
- ¼ teaspoon salt
- ¼ teaspoon dried thyme, crushed
- ¼ cup shredded Parmesan cheese, and more for garnish
- Chopped fresh parsley

MAKE IT

1 Cook linguine according to the package directions; drain and set aside.

2 Meanwhile, heat oil on medium in a large skillet. Add garlic; cook 30 seconds. Toss in clams; cook until heated. Mix in pasta, salt, and thyme. Stir in cheese. Transfer to bowls. Top with more cheese and parsley. Makes 4 servings.

Nutrition per serving: 395 calories; 21g protein; 14g fat (3g saturated fat); 45g carbohydrate; 2g fiber; 142mg calcium; 12mg iron; 312mg sodium.

nutrition note

Fresh clams contain the most iron of any food; just one supplies about 2 milligrams of the mineral.

A-B-C Pasta Salad

Since you cook the noodles and veggies at the same time, this vitamin A–packed dish is good to go in 15 minutes. If you're toting it to a picnic, take extra dressing in case the pasta dries out.

INGREDIENTS

- 1 cup whole-grain alphabet-shaped pasta
- ⅔ cup minced carrots
- ½ cup peas
- ½ cup diced part-skim mozzarella cheese
- ¼ cup light Italian or balsamic-vinaigrette salad dressing

MAKE IT

1 Cook pasta according to the package directions. Add the carrots and peas during the last minute of cooking. Drain and rinse with cold water.

2 In a large bowl with a lid, gently mix together the pasta, vegetables, mozzarella cheese, and salad dressing. Makes 6 toddler-size servings.

Nutrition per serving: 101 calories; 5g protein; 3g fat (1g saturated fat); 14g carbohydrate; 1g fiber; 80mg calcium; 1mg iron; 173mg sodium.

cooking fun

Challenge your child to pick out ingredients from the pantry: "Quick, find me something that begins with the letter S." And when she brings you a box of spaghetti have her point out the word "spaghetti." All the while, she's honing her prereading skills, and you have someone to find everything you need to get dinner on the table.

Simple Shrimp Alfredo

If your child likes veggies in cheese sauce, she'll go for this speedy dinner.

INGREDIENTS

- 8 ounces spinach fettuccine
- 1 package (16 ounces) frozen Italian-blend vegetables
- ½ jar (16 ounces) reduced-fat Alfredo sauce
- 8 ounces peeled, cooked medium shrimp (tails removed)
- ¼ cup grated Parmesan cheese, plus additional if desired
- 2 tablespoons fresh lemon juice

MAKE IT

1 Cook pasta according to the directions on the package. Five minutes before it's done, stir the vegetables into the pot.

2 Drain, reserving ½ cup of the cooking liquid. Return pasta and veggies to the pot. Stir in Alfredo sauce, reserved cooking liquid, shrimp, cheese, and lemon juice and cook until warm.

3 Sprinkle with additional cheese before serving, if you like. Makes 6 servings.

Nutrition per serving: 309 calories; 19g protein; 8g fat (4g saturated fat); 38g carbohydrate; 5g fiber; 190mg calcium; 3mg iron; 609mg sodium.

Toddler Veggie Pasta

The pasta and veggies contain folic acid, a B vitamin that is important during pregnancy and childhood.

INGREDIENTS

- 1 cup acini de pepe or pastina
- ⅓ cup finely diced carrots
- ⅓ cup finely diced red bell pepper
- ⅓ cup frozen baby peas
- ⅓ cup finely chopped broccoli
- ⅓ cup frozen whole-kernel corn
- 1 tablespoon olive oil
- ⅛ teaspoon pepper

MAKE IT

Cook pasta in lightly salted boiling water for 7 minutes. Stir in veggies and cook for 5 minutes; drain. Mix in oil and pepper. Makes 6 toddler-size servings.

Nutrition per serving: 180 calories; 6g protein; 3g fat (0 saturated fat); 32g carbohydrate; 2g fiber; 15mg calcium; 2mg iron; 18mg sodium.

cooking fun

Your toddler can learn these five kitchen skills: Tearing lettuce, steadying a mixing bowl while you pour, washing fruit, handing you a nonbreakable measuring cup, and stirring the ingredients (with your help).

Pistachio Pesto

The spinach is so finely chopped in this recipe that your kid won't even realize what it is.

INGREDIENTS

1	cup packed spinach
⅓	cup olive oil
¼	cup shelled pistachio nuts
¼	cup grated Parmesan cheese
½	teaspoon salt
1	clove garlic, quartered
12	ounces dried pasta, cooked and drained

MAKE IT

Put spinach, oil, nuts, cheese, salt, and garlic in food processor. Process until smooth. Toss with pasta and serve. Makes 6 cups.

Nutrition per cup: 361 calories; 10g protein; 16g fat (3g saturated fat); 44g carbohydrate; 2g fiber; 60mg calcium; 2mg iron; 253mg sodium.

nutrition note

How much sugar is in a forkful of pasta with tomato sauce? Probably a lot more than you think. Some jarred tomato sauces pack three teaspoons of the sweet stuff into each half cup—and most of it is added during processing. Look for sauces with no more than 5 grams of sugar and 350 milligrams of sodium per ½-cup serving.

Taco Casserole

This zesty dish has just enough spice to be interesting but not too much to intimidate developing palates.

INGREDIENTS

- 1 pound lean ground beef
- 1 can (19 ounces) no-salt-added black beans with liquid
- 1 can (14.5 ounces) no-salt-added diced tomatoes
- 1 package (1.25 ounces) reduced-sodium taco seasoning
- 1 pouch (6.5 ounces) cornbread mix
- 2 eggs
- ⅓ cup low-fat milk
- 1 tablespoon vegetable oil
- ½ cup reduced-fat cheddar cheese

MAKE IT

1 Heat oven to 425°F. In a large ovenproof skillet, cook beef over medium heat until browned. Drain fat if necessary. Stir in black beans, tomatoes, and taco seasoning. Bring mixture to a boil over high heat. Cook 1 minute. Transfer to a 9x13 baking dish.

2 Prepare cornbread according to package directions using eggs, milk, and oil in the amounts shown in the ingredients list. Spoon cornbread onto hot taco mixture. Bake 15 minutes. Sprinkle top with cheese and continue baking 5 minutes or until cornbread is golden brown. Let cool 5 minutes before serving. Makes 6 servings.

Nutrition per serving: 334 calories; 21g protein; 14g fat (5g saturated fat); 32g carbohydrate; 5g fiber; 160mg calcium; 3mg iron; 623mg sodium.

Easy Turkey Stromboli

These pizza-crust wraps are fun for kids to eat, and they offer a boost of protein and iron. Spinach gives this meal all the vitamin A that kids need in a day.

INGREDIENTS

- 1 pound turkey-breast tenderloins, cut into strips
- 1 package (11 ounces) refrigerated pizza crust
- 1 cup pasta sauce, divided
- 1 package (10 ounces) frozen chopped spinach, thawed and well drained
- ½ cup shredded Colby and Monterey Jack cheese blend
- 2 teaspoons low-fat milk
- 2 teaspoons grated Parmesan cheese

MAKE IT

1 Heat oven to 400°F. Boil 1 cup of water on medium in a large skillet; add turkey and return to boiling. Cover; simmer 8 to 10 minutes. Allow to cool slightly, then chop.

2 Unroll crust into a 14×12-inch rectangle on a parchment paper–lined baking sheet. Spoon half the sauce down the center, lengthwise, leaving 3 inches on either side. Layer spinach, turkey, and cheese over sauce. Cut 12 strips on both sides of crust. Fold strips over filling, so they overlap. Brush with milk and sprinkle with Parmesan.

3 Bake for 12 minutes. Serve with remaining sauce. Makes 6 servings.

Nutrition per serving: 305 calories; 27g protein; 8g fat (3g saturated fat); 31g carbohydrate; 2g fiber; 157mg calcium; 3mg iron; 553mg sodium.

kitchen tip

If you forgot to thaw the spinach in the fridge, microwave it on high for 2 minutes, then press out the water in a colander.

Apple-Cinnamon Pork Roast with Warm Slaw

Kids love this flavor combo with cereals and desserts—why not give it a shot with this slow-cooker pork too?

INGREDIENTS

- 1 2½- to 3-pound boneless pork-loin roast
- 1 teaspoon dried thyme
- ½ teaspoon kosher salt
- ¼ teaspoon black pepper
- 1 tablespoon vegetable oil
- 1 medium sweet onion, cut into thin wedges
- ½ cup pasteurized apple cider or apple juice
- 2 Jonagold or McIntosh apples, cored and thinly sliced
- 1 tablespoon lemon juice
- ½ teaspoon ground cinnamon
- 1 bag (16 ounces) coleslaw mix

MAKE IT

1 Sprinkle the roast with thyme, salt, and pepper. In a large skillet, add oil and brown meat on all sides.

2 Layer the onion on the bottom of your slow cooker. Place roast on top and pour on the apple cider. If the roast won't fit in your 4- to 5-quart slow cooker, trim it and save the pieces for stir-fry later in the week. Cover and cook on high-heat setting for 2 to 2½ hours. Toss apples with lemon juice and cinnamon. Add them and the coleslaw mix to your slow cooker. Cover and heat 10 minutes more.

3 Remove the roast and place it on a platter. Let rest 10 minutes before slicing. Using a slotted spoon, transfer the vegetables and apple slices to the platter. Drizzle any remaining cooking juices over meat and vegetables. Makes 8 servings.

Nutrition per serving: 372 calories; 29g protein; 13g fat (7g saturated fat); 13g carbohydrate; 3g fiber; 47mg calcium; 2mg iron; 197mg sodium.

nutrition note

Help kids break out of a bland rut by sprinkling cinnamon on oatmeal, yogurt, applesauce, squash, or sweet potatoes. A dash of cinnamon goes a long way, and some studies suggest that the spice may help prevent spikes in blood sugar.

Super-Simple Paella

Get cozy with the family by making our speedy, healthy version of paella.

INGREDIENTS

- 2 links chicken sausage (6 ounces)
- 1 tablespoon canola oil
- 1 red pepper
- 1 small onion
- ½ teaspoon ground turmeric
  Pinch of salt
- 1 8.8-ounce package cooked brown rice (1½ cups)
- ¼ cup low-sodium chicken broth
- 8 ounces cooked peeled deveined shrimp

MAKE IT

1 Cut sausage in half lengthwise and slice into pieces. Heat canola oil in a large skillet on medium-high and cook sausage until browned, about 2 minutes.

2 Chop the red pepper and the onion and add to pan with turmeric and salt. Cook, uncovered, until tender, 4 minutes, stirring occasionally.

3 Stir in rice, broth, and shrimp. Cook for 2 minutes more to heat through. Makes 4 servings.

Nutrition per serving: 268 calories; 22g protein; 9g fat (2g saturated fat); 22g carbohydrate; 2g fiber; 28mg calcium; 3mg iron; 381mg sodium.

kitchen tip

Break up the rice as you add it to the skillet; it will heat through quicker.

Sweet & Sour Stir-Fry

You can change up the veggies in this Chinese-inspired dish. Other delish options to try: crinkled carrots, snow peas, and green beans.

INGREDIENTS

- 1 tablespoon vegetable oil
- 2 cups broccoli florets
- 1 medium yellow sweet pepper, cut into strips
- 2 green onions, sliced
- 12 ounces pork tenderloin, cut into 1½-inch pieces
- ½ cup bottled stir-fry sauce
  Hot cooked rice
- 1 medium orange, sliced

MAKE IT

1 In a large nonstick skillet, add oil and cook broccoli, pepper, and onions in hot oil over medium-high heat for 4 minutes or until crisp-tender. Transfer from the skillet to a medium bowl.

2 Add pork to skillet and stir-fry for 2 to 3 minutes or until done. You may need to add a few drops of oil to prevent sticking. Return the vegetables to skillet; add sauce. Stir to coat and heat through. Serve over rice garnished with orange slices. Makes 6 servings.

Nutrition per serving: 139 calories; 14g protein; 4g fat (1g saturated fat); 12g carbohydrate; 2g fiber; 46mg calcium; 1mg iron; 735mg sodium.

nutrition note

Did you know that red and yellow peppers offer more vitamin C than citrus fruits? Dip raw pieces in hummus or use them in place of green peppers, which can taste bitter.

French Stew

Will your kids love the crunchy bread-crumb coating on top? *Mais oui!*

INGREDIENTS

- 2 tablespoons olive oil, divided
- 1 pound pork tenderloin, cut into 1½-inch cubes
- 1 medium onion, chopped
- 2 cloves garlic, minced
- 2 cans (15 ounces) cannellini beans, rinsed and drained
- 4 medium carrots, peeled and cut into 1-inch chunks
- 1 can (14 ounces) low-sodium chicken broth
- 1 teaspoon rosemary, crushed
- ¼ teaspoon black pepper
- 4 slices crusty French bread, torn
- Cooked green beans, optional

MAKE IT

1 Heat oven to 375°F. In a 4-quart Dutch oven, heat 1 tablespoon oil over medium-high heat. Add pork, onion, and garlic. Cook and stir until pork is browned, about 4 minutes.

2 Stir in beans, carrots, broth, rosemary, and pepper. Bring to a boil. Cover and bake for 25 minutes. Meanwhile, chop bread in a food processor to form about 1½ cups of coarse crumbs. Toss crumbs with remaining olive oil; sprinkle over meat mixture. Bake, uncovered, 20 minutes more or until pork is cooked and carrots are tender.

3 Serve in shallow bowls with green beans, if desired. Makes 6 servings.

Nutrition per serving: 301 calories; 27g protein; 8g fat (2g saturated fat); 37g carbohydrate; 9g fiber; 68mg calcium; 3mg iron; 467mg sodium.

Chuck-Wagon Pot Roast & Veggies

Even lean cuts of beef become especially tender in the slow cooker.

INGREDIENTS

Nonstick cooking spray

2 to 2½ pounds beef chuck roast
Salt and pepper

1 jar (26 ounces) pasta sauce

1 cup water

2 cups mini wagon-wheel pasta

1 cup baby carrots, halved diagonally

1 cup fresh or frozen cut green beans

MAKE IT

1 Coat a 4-quart slow cooker with cooking spray; set aside. Season beef with salt and pepper. Place beef in the slow cooker. Add sauce and water. Cover; cook on low-heat setting for 8 hours or high-heat setting for 4 hours.

2 Add pasta, carrots, and green beans, stirring into liquid. If cooking on low, increase heat to high and cook 45 minutes more. Cut beef into bite-size pieces. Makes 8 cups.

Nutrition per cup: 275 calories; 29g protein; 7g fat (2g saturated fat); 23g carbohydrate; 3g fiber; 92mg calcium; 4mg iron; 460mg sodium.

Pork Pozole

If you're tired of tacos, try this Mexican dish made with hominy, a type of corn. As it simmers in the slow cooker, you can get some work done—or sit down and read a story.

INGREDIENTS

- 1 can (15 ounces) yellow or white hominy, drained
- 1 can (14.5 ounces) Mexican-style no-salt-added diced tomatoes
- 1 can (10 ounces) mild green enchilada sauce
- 1 large onion, chopped
- 3 cloves garlic, minced
- 2 teaspoons ground cumin
- 1½ pounds boneless pork loin
- ½ cup chopped cilantro
- 1 tablespoon lime juice
  Baked tortilla chips
  Diced avocado and lime wedges, optional

MAKE IT

1 Combine the hominy, tomatoes, enchilada sauce, onion, garlic, and cumin in a 4-quart slow cooker. Top with pork, spooning hominy mixture over the meat. Cover and cook on high-heat setting for 2 to 2½ hours.

2 Place pork on a cutting board. Add cilantro and lime juice to the slow cooker. Coarsely chop pork; return to cooker, and stir well. Spoon into shallow bowls. Serve with tortilla chips, and if your family likes avocado and lime wedges, include them too. Makes 6 servings.

Nutrition per serving: 371 calories; 24g protein; 16g fat (5g saturated fat); 29g carbohydrate; 4g fiber; 55mg calcium; 2mg iron; 396mg sodium.

cooking fun

It's easy to create "passport meals" right in your kitchen: Play music from the country the dish comes from while you cook, and talk about the language and culture of the country with your child. Pair this pork dinner with mariachi music!

Beef & Barley Stew

Even kids who fuss over food will go for the barley in this slow-cooker dish, because the beef broth and seasonings make it amazingly flavorful.

INGREDIENTS

- 1 pound lean beef stew meat (1 to 1½-inch cubes)
- 1 tablespoon vegetable oil
- 1 package (32 ounces) low-sodium beef broth
- 2 cups baby carrots
- ½ package (16 ounces) frozen pearl onions (1¾ cups)
- 2 stalks celery, sliced
- 1 cup water
- ¾ cup pearl barley
- ½ teaspoon pumpkin-pie spice
- ¼ teaspoon ground black pepper
- ¼ cup chopped fresh parsley

MAKE IT

1 In a large skillet, brown stew meat in hot oil over medium-high heat. Then transfer to your 4-quart slow cooker. Stir in all of the remaining ingredients except the parsley.

2 Cover and cook on low-heat setting for 9 to 10 hours or on high-heat setting for 4½ to 5 hours. If you want the broth to be a little thinner, stir in ¼ cup of water at a time until it reaches the consistency you like. Spoon the stew into bowls and sprinkle with parsley. Makes 8 servings.

Nutrition per serving: 182 calories; 16g protein; 4g fat (1g saturated fat); 20g carbohydrate; 4g fiber; 29mg calcium; 2mg iron; 144mg sodium.

kitchen tip

Be sure to get pearl barley—not quick-cooking barley—for this stew. Pearl barley has had the bran removed and has been steamed and polished. It will remain pleasingly chewy over the long cooking time— quick-cooking barley would get mushy.

Tuscan Chicken with Artichokes

Head off complaints from your picky eaters by serving their meal with egg noodles rather than couscous. Adding the fresh vegetables to the slow cooker for just 15 minutes of cooking time ensures they'll be crisp-tender, not mushy.

INGREDIENTS

- 2 packages (9 ounces each) frozen artichoke hearts, defrosted and divided
- 1 medium onion, chopped
- 3 cloves garlic, minced
- 1 can (14 ounces) low-sodium chicken broth
- 2 pounds skinless, boneless chicken thighs
- 1 teaspoon Mediterranean or Greek seasoning
- ½ teaspoon kosher salt
- ¼ teaspoon ground black pepper
- 1 medium zucchini, sliced
- 1 cup halved grape tomatoes
- 1 package (11 ounces) dry whole-wheat couscous
- Chopped parsley, optional

MAKE IT

1 In a 3½- or 4-quart slow cooker, combine one package of artichoke hearts, onion, garlic, and broth. Add chicken and sprinkle it with Mediterranean seasoning, salt, and pepper. Cover and cook on high-heat setting for 3 hours. Then place zucchini, tomatoes, and second package of artichokes in the cooker; re-cover and cook for another 15 minutes, or until veggies are cooked.

2 Remove chicken and vegetables with a slotted spoon; cover them with foil to keep warm. Stir the couscous into the remaining liquid. Cover and cook 5 minutes, or until the liquid is absorbed. Fluff couscous with a fork. Serve chicken and vegetables over couscous. Top with parsley, if desired. Makes 6 servings.

Nutrition per serving: 445 calories; 43g protein; 7g fat (2g saturated fat); 56g carbohydrate; 12g fiber; 79mg calcium; 4mg iron; 383mg sodium.

nutrition note

The list of nutrients in zucchini is impressive: fiber, manganese, vitamin C, magnesium, beta-carotene, potassium, folate, copper, and riboflavin. Grill slices and top with balsamic vinegar or Italian dressing, or swap zucchini for potatoes when cooking potato pancakes.

Easy Indian Curry

If your kids haven't eaten the healthiest breakfast or lunch, this one-pot slow cooker dish can make up for it: A serving delivers major fiber and lots of protein.

INGREDIENTS

- 2 teaspoons olive oil
- 1 medium onion, chopped
- 2 tablespoons tomato paste
- 1½ tablespoons curry powder
- ½ teaspoon cinnamon
- ½ teaspoon salt
- 3 cloves garlic, chopped
- 2 teaspoons grated ginger
- 1 pound dried yellow split peas
- 6 cups water
- ¾ pound small red potatoes, quartered
- 2 cups frozen green peas
- 2 tablespoons cream of coconut (not coconut milk)
- Chopped fresh cilantro, optional

MAKE IT

1 In a saucepan, heat oil on high. Add onion and cook for 3 minutes. Stir in the tomato paste, curry, cinnamon, salt, garlic, and ginger and cook for just 2 minutes.

2 Transfer the onion mixture to a 4-quart slow cooker. Stir in the split peas, the water, and potatoes. Cook on low-heat setting for 8 to 9 hours or on high-heat setting for 3 to 4 hours. About 15 minutes before you're ready to serve, stir in the green peas and cream of coconut. Spoon into bowls; sprinkle on cilantro, if desired. Makes 8 servings.

Nutrition per serving: 292 calories; 17g protein; 3g fat (1g saturated fat); 52g carbohydrate; 18g fiber; 63mg calcium; 4mg iron; 236mg sodium.

kitchen tip

A little bit of bread to dip in this stew makes it all the more appealing. Try whole-grain naan—an Indian flatbread that is available in the bread aisle of most supermarkets.

Greens & Beans

The cornbread bakes, conveniently, while you're making the beans-and-green dish on the stove top.

INGREDIENTS

- 1 package (8.5 ounces) corn muffin mix
- 1 tablespoon olive oil
- 1 red sweet pepper, chopped
- 3 cloves garlic, minced
- 2 15-ounce cans Great Northern beans, rinsed and drained
- 1 package (10 ounces) frozen chopped spinach, thawed and drained
- ½ cup low-sodium chicken broth
- ½ cup water
- 2 tablespoons finely shredded Parmesan cheese
  Cracked black pepper

MAKE IT

1 Prepare the corn muffin mix according to the directions on the package, but place the batter in a greased 8-inch-square pan. Bake at 400°F for 15 minutes, or until golden.

2 In the meantime, heat the oil on medium-high in a large skillet. Add red pepper and garlic; cook for about 4 minutes, stirring occasionally.

3 Mix in the canned beans. Add spinach, chicken broth, and the water; bring to a boil. Cook, uncovered, for 3 to 4 minutes or until most of the liquid has evaporated.

4 Put in bowls and top each portion with cheese and black pepper. Slice half of the cornbread and serve on the side. Wrap the rest for the next day. Makes 4 servings.

Nutrition per serving (with corn bread) : 335 calories; 19g protein; 8g fat (1g saturated fat); 55g carbohydrate; 11g fiber; 172mg calcium; 4mg iron; 775mg sodium.

kitchen tip

Any white bean works just fine in this dish. If you don't have Great Northern beans, you can use cannellini or navy beans.

snacks & drinks

QUICK BITES • SWEET SIPS

Your kids aren't dull, so why should their food be? Jazz up **nutritious basics** like juice, fruit, and beans in these **easy ways,** and watch kids **dig in** with gusto.

Six-Layer Mexican Dip

Don't have a meat eater? All varieties of beans supply nearly as much iron and protein as beef and they're packed with fiber so kids stay full.

INGREDIENTS

- 2 avocados chopped
- 3 tablespoons lemon juice
- 1 clove garlic, minced
- ¼ teaspoon salt
- ⅛ teaspoon pepper
- 1 15-ounce can black beans, rinsed and drained
- 1 15-ounce can Great Northern or cannellini beans, rinsed and drained
- ¾ cup salsa
- 1 cup light sour cream
- ⅓ cup shredded reduced-fat cheddar cheese
- 6 8-inch warmed whole-grain flour or corn tortillas, cut into triangles

MAKE IT

1 Place avocados, lemon juice, garlic, salt, and pepper in a bowl and mash with a spatula.

2 In a 6-cup clear glass bowl, spread black beans in an even layer. Top with avocado mixture, then Great Northern beans, salsa, sour cream, and cheese. Cover and chill up to 24 hours. Spoon the dip onto tortillas. Makes 6 servings.

Nutrition per serving: 378 calories; 19g protein; 16g fat (5g saturated fat); 41g carbohydrate; 19g fiber; 244mg calcium; 4mg iron; 519mg sodium

nutrition note

Rinsing canned beans washes away up to 40 percent of added salt.

Fun Focaccia

These easy pizza squares make a great snack, lunch, or party food.

INGREDIENTS

- 1 tube (13.8 ounces) refrigerated pizza dough
- 1 pint grape tomatoes, cut into halves
- 1 garlic clove, minced
- ½ teaspoon salt
- ¼ teaspoon Italian seasoning
- ½ cup shredded Parmesan

MAKE IT

1 Heat oven to 400°F. Unroll and slightly stretch dough onto a greased baking sheet.

2 Combine tomatoes, garlic, salt, and seasoning in a microwave-safe bowl. Cover and microwave on high for 3 minutes. Let cool another 5 minutes and drain off liquid.

3 Sprinkle dough with Parmesan. Top with tomato mixture. Bake 20 to 22 minutes or until crisp and browned. Let cool 5 minutes, then cut into 12 squares and serve. Makes 12 servings.

Nutrition per serving: 87 calories; 3g protein; 2g fat (1g saturated fat); 13g carbohydrate; 1g fiber; 48mg calcium; 1mg iron; 259mg sodium.

cooking fun

While you're making a homemade piecrust, bread, or other dough without eggs, tear off a small piece of dough and give it to your kid to squish around, pat into her own pretend pie, or make mini sculptures. It'll keep her busy and happy while you're cooking.

Princess Tea Sandwiches

The perfect treat for your next playdate or preschooler birthday party.

INGREDIENTS

- 12 slices whole-grain party rye bread
- ½ cup light semisoft cheese with garlic and herbs
- 1 pear, cored and sliced
- 1 tablespoon lemon juice
- ¼ cup strawberry preserves, fruit spread, or jam

MAKE IT

Spread bread with cheese. Brush pear slices with lemon juice to prevent them from turning brown. Top cheese with preserves, then place 2 slices of pear to create a heart shape. If necessary, trim the rounded end of each pear slice to resemble a heart. Makes 12 open-face sandwiches.

Nutrition per sandwich: 67 calories; 2g protein; 3g fat (1g saturated fat); 9g carbohydrate; 1g fiber; 28mg calcium; 0mg iron; 117mg sodium.

nutrition note

Most rye bread is not whole grain, so check labels carefully.

Smart Snacks

Helping to make these tasty little bites will keep your child occupied. Eating them will fill him up—and provide good nutrition too.

← Fruit & Cheese Kabobs

Perfect for parties or preschool, you can make these snacks-on-a stick and store them in the refrigerator for up to 24 hours.

MAKE IT

Use assorted 1- to 1½-inch cookie cutters to cut shapes out of cantaloupe and honeydew slices and 2 ounces reduced-fat cheddar cheese. Thread melon and cheese on four small skewers along with mixed berries. Place in a flat container; cover. Makes 4 kabobs.

Nutrition per kabob: 50 calories; 4g protein; 3g fat (2g saturated fat); 3g carbohydrate; 1g fiber; 204mg calcium; 0mg iron; 122mg sodium.

← Monarch Munchies

If you don't have currants, just chop up raisins.

MAKE IT

Spread 8 Pepperidge Farm butterfly crackers with 4 teaspoons red-pepper hummus. Arrange 2 teaspoons currants on top as shown. Makes 8 crackers.

Nutrition per cracker: 26 calories; 0g protein; 1g fat (0g saturated fat); 4g carbohydrate; 0g fiber; 0mg calcium; 0mg iron; 38mg sodium.

SAY YES TO
SNACKS

Kids need to have snacks between meals. Their stomachs are small, so the fuel they consume at breakfast, lunch, and supper disappears quickly. They're also growing and physically active. Choosing bites based on fruits, vegetables, and lean proteins is the key to smart snacking.

← Starry Chocolate Fruit

Chocolate is actually packed with heart-healthy antioxidants.

MAKE IT

Cut 10 star and/or moon shapes from kiwifruit and mangoes. Pat fruit with paper towels to remove excess moisture. Melt 1½ ounces bittersweet chocolate in a small bowl by microwaving on medium for 1 to 2 minutes, stirring once or twice. Dip half of each fruit into the chocolate, or let kids do it themselves. Makes 10 pieces.

Nutrition per one kiwi and one star: 27 calories; 0g protein; 2g fat (1g saturated fat); 4g carbohydrate; 1g fiber; 4mg calcium; 0mg iron; 0mg sodium.

Pear-Bear Muffins

Your kids will go wild for this healthy after-school snack.

INGREDIENTS

- 1 package (18.25 ounces) spice cake mix
- 1 cup water
- ⅓ cup orange juice
- 2 eggs
- ¼ cup canola oil
- 2 to 3 pears, cored, and cut into 48 slices
  Almond slivers
  Semisweet chocolate chips, regular and mini

MAKE IT

1 Heat oven to 400°F. Line 2½-inch muffin cups with baking wrappers. In a large bowl, whisk together cake mix, the water, orange juice, eggs, and oil until smooth. Spoon batter into prepared cups until they're about two-thirds full.

2 Trim ½ inch from the pointed end of each pear slice. Insert the trimmed, flat ends of 2 slices into each muffin cup, leaving the tops of the pears exposed. Pretending the muffin is a clock, insert them at about 11:00 and 1:00.

3 Bake for 20 minutes, or until muffin tops spring back when you touch them. Let cool 5 minutes in the pan; remove muffins and place them on wire racks. While they're slightly warm, add almond slivers and chocolate chips to create the bear's face. Makes about 24 muffins.

Nutrition per muffin: 139 calories; 1g protein; 5g fat (1g saturated fat); 22g carbohydrate; 1g fiber; 46mg calcium; 1mg iron; 147mg sodium.

Mini Nacho Cups

These nacho bowls are perfect for movie night with the family. Ask your kids to help you make them.

INGREDIENTS

18 Tostitos Scoops! baked
     tortilla chips

½   15-ounce can black beans,
     rinsed and drained

⅓   cup salsa

½   cup shredded, reduced-fat
     cheddar cheese

⅓   cup reduced-fat sour cream

MAKE IT

1 Heat oven to 350°F. Place chips in a baking dish.

2 In a small saucepan, combine the black beans and salsa and heat on medium. Spoon some of the mixture into the center of each chip.

3 Sprinkle on cheese. Then pop the chips into the oven for about 5 minutes, or until the cheese melts. Put the nachos on a plate and add a dollop of sour cream. Makes 18 nacho cups.

Nutrition per 3 nacho cups: 128 calories; 6g protein; 6g fat (2g saturated fat); 13g carbohydrate; 3g fiber; 135mg calcium; 1mg iron; 206mg sodium.

Pretzel Trio

These super-easy, twisty treats look like the versions at the carnival or shopping mall, but the whole-wheat dough makes them much healthier.

INGREDIENTS

All-purpose flour

1 pound frozen whole-wheat bread dough, thawed

1 egg

¼ cup sesame seeds

¼ cup cinnamon sugar

¼ cup grated Parmesan cheese

MAKE IT

1 Place bread dough on a floured cutting board and roll it into a rectangle. You want it to be about 12×10 inches. Slice the dough lengthwise into 12 strips with a pizza cutter.

2 Make each dough strip into a loop. Flip back the ends of the loop, crossing them to create the twist. Transfer to a lined cookie sheet; cover and allow to rise for 20 minutes.

3 Heat oven to 400°F. Whisk egg and 1 tablespoon water. Brush pretzels with egg mixture and top with sesame seeds, cinnamon sugar, or cheese. Bake 15 minutes, or until browned. Cool on a wire rack. Makes 12 pretzels.

Nutrition per pretzel: 108 calories; 5g protein; 2g fat (0g saturated fat); 18g carbohydrate; 2g fiber; 12mg calcium; 0mg iron; 216mg sodium.

cooking fun ● ● ● ●

Kids love to play with water. Set your child up at the sink so he can fill and empty different-size plastic containers—he'll be learning about the concept of volume. Add small objects like measuring spoons and rubber spatulas so he can guess: Float or sink? Squirt in a little dish soap so he can "observe" the bubbles and count how long it takes them to pop.

Cheese Fondue

Healthy doses of bone-building calcium and muscle- and brain-building protein are served up in a bowl of creamy, cheesy sauce. Dipping is so much fun!

INGREDIENTS

- 1 tablespoon butter
- 1 tablespoon all-purpose flour
- 1 cup fat-free or low-fat milk
- 12 ounces reduced-fat cheddar cheese, shredded (3 cups)
- Vegetables, cooked meat, or pasta, for dipping

MAKE IT

In a medium fondue pot or saucepan, melt butter over medium heat. Add flour and whisk until combined and smooth. Add milk to saucepan. Cook and stir until thickened and bubbly. Reduce heat to medium-low. Gradually add cheese, stirring until melted. Serve with vegetables, cooked meat, or pasta for dipping. Makes 2 cups (16 servings).

Nutrition per 2-tablespoon serving (without dippers): 73 calories; 6g protein; 5g total fat (3g saturated fat); 2g carbohydrate; 0g dietary fiber; 211mg calcium; 1mg iron; 167mg sodium.

Fruity Punch

Serve this virgin version of Sangria at your kid's next party.

INGREDIENTS

- 4½ cups 100% fruit-juice punch
- 1½ cups cranberry juice
- 1½ cups pomegranate juice
- ⅓ cup orange juice
- ½ cup sliced plums
- ½ cup orange wedges
- ½ cup grapes (slice for kids under 4)

MAKE IT

Combine all four kinds of juice in a large pitcher. Add the fruit slices and stir. Makes 8 servings.

Nutrition per serving: 142 calories; 1g protein; 0 fat (0 saturated fat); 35g carbohydrate; 1g fiber; 29mg calcium; 1mg iron; 10mg sodium.

kitchen tip

When packing drinks for school lunch, swap hard-to-puncture juice pouches for juice boxes or milk cartons, or pick up a no-spill, reusable sports bottle. Open store-bought bottles to break the seal. The cafeteria volunteers will thank you!

Moo-riffic Milk

Sure, kids love milk, but at snacktime, try jazzing up the plain stuff with fruit, cocoa, and other fun flavors. Warm or cold, these milk-based creations are sure bets.

← Peach Parfait

Because it contains two servings of fruit, this parfait will be just peachy for breakfast.

MAKE IT

Mix 1 cup fresh sliced peaches, 1½ cups low-fat or fat-free milk, and ⅛ teaspoon almond extract in a blender until smooth. Mash 1 cup raspberries with a fork. Layer milk mixture and raspberries in two glasses. Makes 2 servings.

Nutrition per serving: 140 calories; 8g protein; 2g fat (1g saturated fat); 24g carbohydrate; 5g fiber; 248mg calcium; 1mg iron; 81mg sodium.

← Minty Chocolate Milk

Here's a drinkable version of meltaway mints.

MAKE IT

Place 1½ cups low-fat or fat-free milk, 2 tablespoons dark-chocolate-flavored syrup, and ⅛ teaspoon peppermint extract in a small pitcher. Whisk until combined. In the microwave, melt a few chocolate chips on 2 graham crackers. Divide milk between two glasses. Makes 2 servings.

Nutrition per serving: 132 calories; 7g protein; 2g fat (1g saturated fat); 21g carbohydrate; 1g fiber; 232mg calcium; 1mg iron; 94mg sodium.

DRINK IT UP

If your 4- to 8-year old kid is a milk lover, it's no sweat for her to get the 800 milligrams of calcium she needs daily for strong bones and teeth (or 500mg, if she's between 1 and 3). Otherwise, focus on low-fat yogurt and cheese, or up to 6 ounces of fortified 100% fruit juice. Look for brands that have vitamin D; it helps kids absorb calcium.

← Peppermint Fluff

A "fluff" is simply frothed milk—think a junior latte without the caffeine, of course.

MAKE IT

Warm 1 cup of low-fat milk on medium for 5 to 10 minutes. Mix in a few drops of peppermint extract. Break a candy cane into a couple of small pieces and chop it with a sharp knife. Whisk milk in the blender for 2 minutes or use a frother. Pour into two cups and top with crushed peppermint. Makes 2 servings.

Nutrition per serving: 80 calories; 4g protein; 1g fat (1g saturated fat); 13g carbohydrate; 0g fiber; 156mg calcium; 0mg iron; 56mg sodium.

Healthy Shirley Temples

This kiddie cocktail is on tap. Using fresh, in-season Bing cherries and real juice, you can create a drink that's just 40 calories a cup (regular ones are, gulp, around 150).

INGREDIENTS

- 8 fresh Bing cherries
- 1½ cups seltzer
- ¼ cup cherry juice

MAKE IT

1 Fill two glasses about halfway with ice and put 4 cherries in each.

2 In a pitcher, mix seltzer and cherry juice.

3 Pour seltzer mixture into glasses and offer to kids 4 and over. Slice the cherries for younger kids. Makes 2 cups.

Nutrition per cup: 40 calories; 0g protein; 0g fat (0g saturated fat); 9g carbohydrate; 1g fiber; 4mg calcium; 0mg iron; 3mg sodium.

kitchen tip

In most of the country, cherry season starts in June. Don't miss the chance to get the fruit at its best flavor—and best price.

Pomegranate Smoothie

Think your kid is getting sick? Whip up this drink with pomegranate juice, a potent flu-fighter.

INGREDIENTS

- 1 cup pomegranate juice
- 6 ounces low-fat vanilla yogurt
- 2 tablespoons honey
- ½ cup ice
- Pomegranate seeds

MAKE IT

In a blender, mix juice, yogurt, and honey until smooth. Add ice; blend until frothy. Divide between two glasses; sprinkle with pomegranate seeds. Makes 2 smoothies.

Nutrition per smoothie: 210 calories; 5g protein; 2g fat (1g saturated fat); 47g carbohydrate; 1g fiber; 162mg calcium; 0mg iron; 69mg sodium.

kitchen tip ● ● ● ●

You can buy pomegranate seeds solo at most supermarkets. But it's much more fun to remove your own from the fruit. Just cut off the crown of the pomegranate, then score with a knife, top to bottom, around the fruit, taking care not to cut all of the way through. Place the fruit, top side down, into a bowl of cold water; let it soak for 5 to 10 minutes. Break the fruit apart into the bowl of water. The seeds should sink to the bottom. Remove the shell with a slotted spoon, then drain the seeds in a colander. Pat them dry with a clean paper towel. Eat immediately or store in a sealed container in the fridge for up to 2 days.

treats

COOKIES • CUPCAKES • FRUIT DESSERTS

Healthy diets include **dessert!** From perfectly proportioned everyday goodies to treats for **kids' birthdays** and holidays, follow our simple path to sweet serenity.

Peanut-Butter Cookies

With just three ingredients, this may be the simplest cookie recipe ever!

INGREDIENTS

- 1 cup peanut butter, smooth or chunky
- 1 cup sugar, plus more for rolling
- 1 egg

MAKE IT

1 Heat oven to 375°F. Stir together all ingredients in a large mixing bowl.

2 Roll dough into 1-inch balls. Put some sugar on a plate and roll balls in it to coat. Place 2 inches apart on ungreased cookie sheets.

3 Press each ball down with a fork to make a crisscross design. Bake for 10 minutes or until cookies just start to brown on the edges. Remove from the oven and let cool on wire racks. Makes 24 cookies.

Nutrition per cookie: 102 calories; 3g protein; 6g fat (1g saturated fat); 12g carbohydrate; 1g fiber; 6mg calcium; 0mg iron; 52mg sodium.

kitchen tip

These flourless peanut-butter cookies are bound only by the beaten egg, making them soft and chewy. Serve them with a glass of milk.

Pink Lemonade Cookies

These cookies are made with (surprise!) lemonade mix.

INGREDIENTS

- ½ cup butter, softened
- ½ cup granulated sugar
- ¼ cup powdered lemonade mix
- 1 egg
- 8 drops red food coloring
- 1¾ cups all-purpose flour
  Pinch of salt
- ¼ cup pink decorating sugar
- 1 tablespoon light corn syrup
- 1½ cups powdered sugar
- 2 to 3 tablespoons fresh lemon juice

MAKE IT

1 In a large bowl, combine butter, sugar, and lemonade mix. Beat with a mixer on medium-high speed until fluffy, about 3 minutes. Add egg and food coloring; beat well. Gradually add flour and salt; beat until dough begins to cling.

2 Gather dough into a ball and shape into a 7×2½-inch log. Wrap in wax paper. Chill 3 hours so it's firm enough to slice.

3 Heat oven to 350°F. Line cookie sheets with parchment paper. Place pink sugar in a shallow bowl. Brush outside of the dough log with corn syrup. Cut log crosswise into ⅛-inch-thick slices. Lightly roll the edges of the slices in pink sugar. Place on cookie sheets about 1 inch apart. Cut some cookies in half, if desired. Score the top of cookies with the back of a knife to make them resemble citrus segments.

4 Bake 8 minutes, or until edges are just firm. Let cool on a wire rack.

5 Mix the powdered sugar and lemon juice; place in a resealable plastic bag. Snip a small hole in one corner of the bag. Pipe icing onto scored lines and add dots. Let stand until the icing is set. Makes about 2½ dozen cookies.

Nutrition per cookie: 108 calories; 1g protein; 3g fat (2g saturated fat); 19g carbohydrate; 0g fiber; 5mg calcium; 0mg iron; 32mg sodium.

Carrot Tops

Each yummy cupcake contains a half serving of veggies. Without the frosting, they're healthy enough for everyday eating!

INGREDIENTS

Cupcakes

2	cups white whole-wheat flour
1	teaspoon baking soda
1	teaspoon cinnamon
½	teaspoon baking powder
½	teaspoon salt
2	large eggs
1¼	cups sugar
½	cup canola oil
¼	cup orange juice
1½	cups grated carrots

Topping

1	package (8 ounces) low-fat cream cheese, softened
4	tablespoons unsalted butter, softened
1	box (16 ounces) confectioners' sugar
3	tablespoons low-fat milk
1	teaspoon vanilla extract
8	graham crackers, crushed
18	circus peanuts
4	green Twizzlers

MAKE IT

1 Heat oven to 350°F. Line 18 muffin cups with paper liners. Combine flour, baking soda, cinnamon, baking powder, and salt in a medium bowl; whisk until blended. In a separate bowl, beat eggs and sugar with a wooden spoon. Add oil and orange juice, then combine with flour mixture. Fold in carrots.

2 Divide batter among prepared liners. Bake 18 to 22 minutes, or until a toothpick inserted into centers come out clean. Transfer to a wire rack and let cool completely.

3 To decorate tops, beat cream cheese and butter until smooth. Gradually add sugar and milk; beat until smooth. Mix in vanilla. Frost cupcakes, then roll edges in crushed graham crackers. Top each with a circus peanut. Poke a few holes in each peanut; insert Twizzler pieces for stem. Makes 18 cupcakes.

Nutrition per cupcake: 364 calories; 4g protein; 13g fat (4g saturated fat); 60g carbohydrate; 2g fiber; 42mg calcium; 1mg iron; 230mg sodium.

195

Monkey Business Cupcakes

What flavor are these cupcakes? Banana, of course! You can use a boxed mix instead of our recipe, but mash real fruit and add it to the batter.

INGREDIENTS

Cupcakes

1⅔ cups white whole-wheat flour
1 teaspoon baking powder
½ teaspoon baking soda
¼ teaspoon salt
1 cup mashed bananas, about 2 large
⅓ cup buttermilk
1 teaspoon vanilla extract
½ cup canola oil
1 cup sugar
2 large eggs
⅔ cup chocolate chips (mini chips are ideal)

Topping

½ cup heavy cream
2 tablespoons light corn syrup
1½ cups chocolate chips
18 gingersnap cookies
18 mini Oreos
1 tube (4.25 ounces) white decorating frosting
36 mini brown M&Ms

MAKE IT

1 Heat oven to 350°F. Line 18 muffin cups. Combine first four ingredients in a large bowl. In another bowl, blend bananas, buttermilk, and vanilla. Beat in oil and sugar. Add eggs, one at a time, beating well after each. Add banana mixture to flour mixture, stirring gently to combine. Stir in chocolate chips.

2 Divide batter among muffin cups. Bake 15 to 20 minutes. Let cool on a wire rack.

3 To decorate, heat cream and corn syrup in a saucepan until mixture begins to boil. Remove from heat; add chocolate chips. Cover; let stand 5 minutes. Stir until smooth. Glaze cupcakes with chocolate. Spoon extra into a plastic bag and refrigerate.

4 Cut gingersnaps to make a mouth. For ears, separate Oreo tops and bottoms and remove filling. Pipe on white frosting for eyes and top with M&Ms. Snip a small corner from bag of chocolate; pipe on hair and nostrils. Makes 18 cupcakes.

Nutrition per cupcake: 364 calories; 4g protein; 18g fat (7g saturated fat); 50g carbohydrate; 3g fiber; 52mg calcium; 2mg iron; 175mg sodium.

Pixie Cakes

Unfrosted angel-food cupcakes have about 70 fewer calories apiece than typical yellow or chocolate ones—and your little fairies will like them every bit as much.

INGREDIENTS

Cupcakes

- 1 box (16 ounces) angel-food cake mix
- ¼ teaspoon almond extract (optional)

Topping

- 2 cups blue candy melts (wilton.com)
- 1 container (.25 ounces) white cake sparkles (wilton.com)
- 1 cup flaked coconut
- 2 tablespoons confectioners' sugar

MAKE IT

1 Heat oven to 350°F. Line 24 muffin cups. Prepare cake mix according to package directions. Stir in almond extract, if desired.

2 Divide batter among muffin cups. Bake 15 to 20 minutes, until puffed and golden. Cool pan on a wire rack.

3 To decorate, line 3 cookie sheets with wax paper. Microwave candy melts on high for 15 seconds. Stir; microwave at 10-second intervals until smooth. Spoon into a heavy resealable bag. Snip a small corner and pipe 24 2½×2-inch pairs of fairy wings onto the sheets, leaving a stem at the bottom to insert into cupcake. Top with sparkles. Refrigerate until set, about 5 minutes.

4 Poke two small holes in the top of each cupcake with a toothpick, and insert wings into cupcakes. Place coconut in between wings and sift on sugar. Makes 24 cupcakes.

Nutrition per cupcake: 175 calories; 2g protein; 6g fat (5g saturated fat); 28g carbohydrate; 1g fiber; 82mg calcium; 0mg iron; 184mg sodium.

kitchen tip

Work quickly when placing the fairy wings on top of each cupcake. Because they're made from melted candy, the warmth from your hands will soften them if you hold them too long.

199

Healthy Desserts

If your child's meals are nutritious, there's no reason to deny her something sweet. These right-sized bites will satisfy her craving, and you can oblige with complete peace of mind.

← Graham-wiches

These simple treats are made with whole-grain graham crackers and low-fat frozen yogurt—healthful and absolutely delicious!

MAKE IT

Spread 3 tablespoons low-fat chocolate, vanilla, or strawberry frozen yogurt between 2 graham-cracker squares. Wrap in plastic and freeze until ready to eat. Makes 1 sandwich.

Nutrition per sandwich: 87 calories; 2g protein; 2g fat (1g saturated fat); 16g carbohydrate; 0g fiber; 23mg calcium; 1mg iron; 106mg sodium.

← Cake Cuties

These party treats look like they came from a bakery, but they're a cinch to make.

MAKE IT

Slice 6 ounces angel-food cake into 20 1½-inch cubes. Stir a few drops red food coloring into 2 cups canned frosting. Microwave frosting on high for 20 seconds, stir, and heat 10 to 15 seconds. Place cubes on a rack and pour over cake. Microwave fruit chews for 10 seconds, until softened. Roll and make shapes with a mini cookie cutter. Place on cakes. Refrigerate until ready to eat. Makes 20 cubes.

Nutrition per cube: 102 calories; 1g protein; 5g fat (1g saturated fat); 14g carbohydrate; 0g fiber; 10mg calcium; 0mg iron; 113mg sodium.

SAVE ROOM

The USDA MyPyramid, the nutrition bible for dietitians, allows children ages 2 to 8 about 165 calories per day for extra calories and fat—aka dessert. The trick is to not blow through all of those calories before the dinner plates are cleared. That way, there will be room for perfectly proportioned desserts prepared with good ingredients—like the ideas shown here.

← Peanut-Butter Balls

Chocolate and peanut butter come together in a homemade version of a favorite candy.

MAKE IT

Mix ½ cup all-natural peanut butter, ⅓ cup honey, and 1 cup powdered milk in a bowl. Roll into 20 1-inch balls. Melt 6 ounces dark chocolate; using a skewer, dip balls in chocolate. Refrigerate until hardened. Pipe on letters with leftover melted chocolate. Makes 20 balls.

Nutrition per ball: 112 calories; 3g protein; 6g fat (2g saturated fat); 12g carbohydrate; 1g fiber; 45mg calcium; 1mg iron; 43mg sodium.

Be-Mine Chocolate Pots

These brownies baked in pots are super-indulgent—save them for a special occasion or share one!

INGREDIENTS

8 ounces semisweet chocolate, chopped

¾ cup butter, sliced

3 large eggs

½ cup granulated sugar

½ teaspoon salt

1 teaspoon vanilla extract

⅔ cup all-purpose flour

Confectioners' sugar

MAKE IT

1 Heat oven to 350°F. Grease eight 6-ounce ramekins and place on a baking pan. In a double boiler, combine chocolate and butter and stir over simmering water until melted. Remove from heat and let cool 5 minutes.

2 In a bowl, whisk eggs, granulated sugar, salt, and vanilla with an electric mixer until frothy, about 2 minutes. Lightly whisk in the chocolate mixture. Fold in flour until combined. Divide mixture among prepared ramekins. Place ramekins on baking sheet in the oven and bake 18 to 22 minutes, or until sides are firm and center is slightly soft. Let cool completely.

3 Place a small heart-shaped stencil or paper with a heart cutout on top of each ramekin. Sprinkle with confectioners' sugar; carefully remove stencil. Makes 8 brownies.

Nutrition per brownie: 407 calories; 5g protein; 28g fat (16g saturated fat); 40g carbohydrate; 2g fiber; 27mg calcium; 2mg iron; 328mg sodium.

kitchen tip

Before decorating, place the confectioners' sugar in a fine-meshed strainer or flour sifter, then gently tap on the side of the strainer. And be sure to decorate right before serving; otherwise, the moisture from the brownie can make the sugar melt and disappear.

Red, White & Blueberries

Cap off a summer barbecue with a spectacular dessert display kids will love.

INGREDIENTS

Nonstick cooking spray
1½ cups berry sorbet
1½ cups coconut or lemon sorbet
1½ cups blue water ice
Blueberries or raspberries

MAKE IT

1 Spritz a loaf pan with nonstick spray and line with plastic wrap overlapping the sides.

2 Spread a 1½-inch layer of softened berry sorbet in the bottom of the pan. Freeze for about 30 minutes. Repeat with layers of coconut or lemon sorbet and blue-water ice or blue ice cream. Cover with plastic wrap and freeze for at least 6 more hours or overnight.

3 Before serving, thaw the loaf on the counter for about 10 minutes, then invert onto a serving tray. Use a knife to make a crisscross design on top, garnish with blueberries or raspberries. Slice and serve immediately. Makes 8 slices.

Nutrition per slice: 130 calories; 0g protein; 0g fat (0g saturated fat); 33g carbohydrate; 1g fiber; 9mg calcium; 0mg iron; 13mg sodium.

kitchen tip

When removing a frozen dessert from a pan, let it stand on the counter for 10 minutes to soften it slightly, or very carefully turn it upside-down and hold it under running lukewarm water for 10 to 15 seconds. It should come out of the pan effortlessly.

Pinwheel Pear Tart

Let your child paint the pastry with milk and then sprinkle on some sugar.

INGREDIENTS

- ¼ cup sugar
- 1 tablespoon all-purpose flour
- 1 teaspoon finely shredded lemon peel
- ¼ teaspoon nutmeg
- 3 pears, cored and sliced
- 1 rolled refrigerated unbaked piecrust
- Milk
- Coarse or granulated sugar

MAKE IT

1 Heat oven to 375°F. Line a baking sheet with parchment paper; set aside.

2 In a large bowl, stir together the sugar, flour, lemon peel, and nutmeg. Add pears and toss to coat.

3 Unroll the piecrust on the prepared baking sheet. Arrange pears, as shown, in a pinwheel shape in the center of the crust, leaving a 1½-inch border of dough exposed. Moving in a clockwise direction, fold the dough toward the center, pleating as necessary. When you're finished, the opening with the pears in the middle should measure about 5 inches wide. Brush the pastry with milk and sprinkle with coarse sugar.

4 Bake tart for about 40 minutes, or until pastry is golden and pears are tender. Serve warm or at room temperature. Makes 8 servings.

Nutrition per serving: 240 calories; 1g protein; 8g fat (3g saturated fat); 40g carbohydrate; 3g fiber; 11mg calcium; 0mg iron; 186mg sodium.

kitchen tip

Pears and apples quickly turn brown when they're cut and exposed to air. To prevent browning, toss the sliced fruit with a small amount of lemon juice. A teaspoon would work in this recipe—the fruit is flavored with lemon peel anyway, so you won't even notice it.

Warm Fruit & Cake Cups

After you get the ingredients together, let the kids assemble this grilled dessert themselves.

INGREDIENTS

- 1 fresh peach
   Nonstick cooking spray
- 3 slices store-bought angel-food cake
- 6 teaspoons raspberry jam
- ⅓ cup raspberries and blueberries
- ⅓ cup light frozen whipped dessert topping, thawed

MAKE IT

Halve the peach; remove pit. Spritz cut sides with nonstick spray. Grill cut sides down on medium heat for 5 minutes or until tender, turning once. Add angel-food cake; grill for 1 minute or until toasted, turning once. Remove and cut peach and cake into bite-size pieces. In six 4- to 6-ounce dessert dishes, layer cake, jam, peaches, berries, and light whipped topping. Makes 6 cups.

Nutrition per cup: 79 calories; 1g protein; 1g fat (1g saturated fat); 16g carbohydrate; 1g fiber; 24mg calcium; 0mg iron; 106mg sodium.

kitchen tip

Grill the peach halves on the outer edge of the barbecue rack so they won't cook so fast and get mushy or blackened.

Blueberry-Nectarine Buckle

Nectarines can be swapped with peaches in almost any recipe, so you can use either type of fruit in this dish.

INGREDIENTS

- 2 cups biscuit mix
- 1 cup sugar, divided
- 1 egg, lightly beaten
- ½ cup reduced-fat milk
- 1 teaspoon finely shredded lemon peel
- 1 medium nectarine, pitted and chopped
- 1¼ cups fresh blueberries
- ½ cup all-purpose flour
- ¼ cup cold butter, cut into cubes

MAKE IT

1 Heat oven to 350°F. Grease the bottom and ½ inch up the sides of a 1½- to 2-quart baking dish. In a medium bowl, combine biscuit mix, ½ cup sugar, egg, milk, and lemon peel. Stir until moistened.

2 Spoon batter into pan. Top with fruit. Mix flour and remaining sugar in a bowl. Using a fork, cut in butter until mixture is crumbly; sprinkle over fruit. Bake for 50 to 60 minutes, or until a toothpick inserted into center comes out clean. Let cool for 30 minutes. Serve warm. Makes 9 servings.

Nutrition per serving: 298 calories; 4g protein; 9g fat (5g saturated fat); 50g carbohydrate; 2g fiber; 51mg calcium; 0mg iron; 390mg sodium.

kitchen tip

What's the difference between a buckle, cobbler, crisp, and crumble? A buckle and a cobbler are nearly the same thing—a deep-dish fruit dessert with a cake-like or sweetened biscuit topping. A crisp and a crumble are likewise similar. Both terms describe a deep-dish fruit dessert with a crumbly pastry topping. It's all good!

Sweet Whole-Wheat Couscous with Almonds & Dried Cherries

It's a healthful take on rice pudding that you can throw together quickly.

INGREDIENTS

- 1½ cups vanilla-flavored almond milk or vanilla-flavored soy milk
- ½ cup water
- ⅛ teaspoon salt
- ¾ cup whole-wheat couscous
- 1 to 2 teaspoons finely shredded orange peel
- ½ cup sliced or chopped almonds (for kids 4 and over)
- ½ cup dried tart cherries, chopped

MAKE IT

1 Put milk, the water, and salt in a medium saucepan over medium-high heat; bring just to boiling (watch carefully so it doesn't boil over). Stir in the couscous and orange peel; remove from heat. Cover and let stand for 5 minutes.

2 Fluff the couscous with a fork. Stir in the almonds and cherries. Serve immediately. Makes 3 cups.

Nutrition per ½ cup: 219 calories; 6g protein; 5g fat (0g saturated fat); 40g carbohydrate; 6g fiber; 120mg calcium; 1mg iron; 92mg sodium.

Strawberry Baskets

Berries are high in vitamin C—which helps the body absorb iron from other foods such as spinach, raisins, peanut butter, and lean red meat.

INGREDIENTS

- 1 package (10 ounces) puff pastry shells
- 1 quart strawberries, hulled and sliced
- 1 tablespoon strawberry preserves
- ¾ cup vanilla ice cream

MAKE IT

1 Heat oven to 400°F. Bake the pastry shells according to the directions on the package. With most brands, you remove the top layer—which becomes a lid—after about 20 minutes and cook the remaining pastry a few minutes longer. Let the pastry cool completely before filling.

2 Meanwhile, mix the strawberry slices with the preserves. If the berries are super-ripe, you probably don't need the preserves.

3 Fill the shells with the strawberry mixture, then microwave ice cream on high for 20 seconds. It won't be entirely melted, but after you stir a few times you'll have a perfect vanilla "cream" sauce. Pour sauce over berries and top with the pastry lid. Makes 6 one-basket servings.

Nutrition per serving: 367 calories; 5g protein; 23g fat (7g saturated fat); 37g carbohydrate; 3g fiber; 52mg calcium; 2mg iron; 136mg sodium.

kitchen tip

If you don't have a strawberry huller, push a plastic straw through the berry from bottom to top to get the job done.

credits

Peter Ardito: Honey-Mustard Chicken Wings, page 90

Iain Bagwell: Peppermint Fluff, page 162, 183

Monica Buck: Citrus-Beef Kabobs, page 79; Child with a rolling pin, page 162; Pretzel Trio, page 177; Cheese Fondue, page 178; Minty Chocolate Milk, page 162, 182; Peach Parfait, page 182; Red, White & Blueberries, page 188, 204

Gemma Comas: Huevos Rancheros, page 8, 12; Sunshine Eggs, page 8, 12; Love Nest, page 13; Tiny Waffle Tower, page 16; Ricotta Cheese Pancakes, page 8, 16; Letter-Perfect Waffles, page 17; Checkerboard Toast, page 8, 22; Chocolate-Milk French Toast, page 22; Jigsaw Puzzle, page 23; Peaches & Cream Smoothie, page 8, 26; Mango Split, page 26; Top Pop, page 27; Child licking his fingers, page 28; Strawberry Soup & PB-and-Raisin Bagel, page 40; Heart-y Pumpernickel & Carrot-Ginger Soup, page 28, 41; Cod Cakes, page 66, 72; Pumpkin Penne, page 125; Cheesy Linguine with Clams, page 129; Six-Layer Mexican Dip, page 162, 164; Graham-wiches, page 188, 200; Cake Cuties, page 200; Peanut-Butter Balls, page 201

Miki Duisterhof: German Pancake with Berries, page 8, 15; Blueberry-Nectarine Buckle, page 210

Jim Franco: BLT in a Bowl, page 28, 47; Kiddie Cobb, page 6, 51; Pinwheel Salad, page 103; Orange Crush, page 66, 104; Be-Mine Chocolate Pots, page 188, 203

Alexandra Grablewski: Healthy Shirley Temples, page 162, 184

Paula Hible: Fast Frittata, page 8, 10; Ravioli & Meatball Soup, page 6, 37; Tandoori Chicken, page 80; Crispy Coconut Chicken, page 66, 83; Moroccan Chicken, page 87; Cauliflower "Popcorn," page 96; Citrusy Edamame, page 96, 217; Greek Stuffed Mushrooms, page 97, 222; Bacon Brussels Sprouts, page 97, 219; Sunny Broccoli, page 108, 221; Minty Peas, page 3, 108; Cucumber Ribbon Salad, page 109; Crinkly Carrot "Fries," page 109; Cheesy Spaghetti Squash, page 116, 220; Honey-Glazed Carrots, page 116; Teriyaki Green Beans, page 117, 223; Breaded Asparagus, page 117; Nutty Noodles, page 127; Simple Shrimp Alfredo, page 66, 132; Toddler Veggie Pasta, page 66, 135; Greens & Beans, page 160; Fruit & Cheese Kabobs, page 162, 170; Monarch Munchies, page 170; Starry Chocolate Fruit, page 171; Strawberry Baskets, page 188, 215

Frances Janisch: Child eating pancake, page 8; Child icing scones, page 8; Chocolate-Hazelnut Pancakes with Raspberry Sauce, page 18; Blueberry Scones, page 24; Child shaking salad, page 28; Watermelon Soup, page 38; Beef & Bean Taco Salad, page 28, 43; Shake-It-Up Salad, page 48; Falafel Pockets, page 64; Fish & Veggies Baked in Parchment, page 75; Pecan-Crusted Fish Sticks, page 77; Caprese Bread Salad, page 107; Pistachio Pesto, page 66, 136; Pomegranate Smoothie, page 187; Pink Lemonade Cookies, page 193; Carrot Tops, page 188, 194; Monkey Business Cupcakes, page 188, 197; Pixie Cakes, page 198

Kang Kim: Banana Quinoa Waffles with Mixed Berries, page 6, 21; Mini Beef & Bulgur Burgers, page 52; Real Popcorn Chicken, page 89; Farotto with Peas & Parmesan, page 112; Sweet Whole-Wheat Couscous with Almonds & Dried Cherries, page 213

Rita Maas: Cheesy Broccoli & Potato Soup, page 30; Black Bean Soup, page 33; Pulled Pork & Pepper Wraps, page 92; Butternut Squash Casserole, page 121; Low-Maintenance Lasagna, page 122; Taco Casserole, page 139; Apple-Cinnamon Pork Roast with Warm Slaw, page 143; Super-Simple Paella, page 66, 145; Chuck-Wagon Pot Roast & Veggies, page 6, 150; Pork Pozole, page 152; Beef & Barley Stew, page 66, 154; Tuscan Chicken with Artichokes, page 156; Easy Indian Curry, page 158

Ericka McConnell: Sandwich Bouquets, page 55; A-B-C Pasta Salad, page 130; Fruity Punch, page 181

Alison Miksch: Greek Kabob Salad, page 28, 44; BBQ Pork Sandwiches, page 28, 56; Indian-Spiced Chicken with Relish, page 84; Spinach & Pear Salad, page 6, 100; Sweet & Sour Stir-Fry, page 147; French Stew, page 149; Princess Tea Sandwiches, page 162, 168; Pear-Bear Muffins, page 6, 173; Pinwheel Pear Tart, page 188, 206

David Prince: Asian Shrimp & Coconut Soup, page 28, 34; Tilapia Piccata, page 71; Healthy Carbonara, page 118

Stephanie Rausser: Family at table, page 5

Alexandra Rowley: Plum-Good Chicken Burgers, page 59; Butterfly Shrimp Skewers, page 6, 68; Rainbow Coleslaw, page 99; Corn & Edamame Salad, page 114; Warm Fruit & Cake Cups, page 6, 209

Lucy Schaeffer: Junior Veggie Burgers, page 28, 63

Josh Titus: Cranberry Pork Chops, page 95; Fun Focaccia, page 162, 167; Mini Nacho Cups, page 162, 174; Child using mixing bowl, page 188; Peanut-Butter Cookies, page 188, 190

Cheryl Zibisky: All-Star Sliders, page 6, 60; Healthy Fried Rice, page 110; Easy Turkey Stromboli, page 140

index

Metric Information

PRODUCT DIFFERENCES

Most of the ingredients called for in the recipes in this book are available in most countries. However, some are known by different names. Here are some common American ingredients and their possible counterparts:

- Sugar (white) is granulated, fine granulated, or castor sugar.
- Powdered sugar is icing sugar.
- All-purpose flour is enriched, bleached or unbleached white household flour. When self-rising flour is used in place of all-purpose flour in a recipe that calls for leavening, omit the leavening agent (baking soda or baking powder) and salt.
- Light-color corn syrup is golden syrup.
- Cornstarch is cornflour.
- Baking soda is bicarbonate of soda.
- Vanilla or vanilla extract is vanilla essence.
- Green, red, or yellow sweet peppers are capsicums or bell peppers.
- Golden raisins are sultanas.

VOLUME AND WEIGHT

The United States traditionally uses cup measures for liquid and solid ingredients. The chart (above right) shows the approximate imperial and metric equivalents. If you are accustomed to weighing solid ingredients, the following approximate equivalents will be helpful.

- 1 cup butter, castor sugar, or rice = 8 ounces = ½ pound = 250 grams
- 1 cup flour = 4 ounces = ¼ pound = 125 grams
- 1 cup icing sugar = 5 ounces = 150 grams
- Canadian and U.S. volume for a cup measure is 8 fluid ounces (237 ml), but the standard metric equivalent is 250 ml.
- 1 British imperial cup is 10 fluid ounces.
- In Australia, 1 tablespoon equals 20 ml, and there are 4 teaspoons in the Australian tablespoon.
- Spoon measures are used for smaller amounts of ingredients. Although the size of the tablespoon varies slightly in different countries, for practical purposes and for recipes in this book, a straight substitution is all that's necessary. Measurements made using cups or spoons always should be level unless stated otherwise.

COMMON WEIGHT RANGE REPLACEMENTS

Imperial / U.S.	Metric
½ ounce	15 g
1 ounce	25 g or 30 g
4 ounces (¼ pound)	115 g or 125 g
8 ounces (½ pound)	225 g or 250 g
16 ounces (1 pound)	450 g or 500 g
1¼ pounds	625 g
1½ pounds	750 g
2 pounds or 2¼ pounds	1,000 g or 1 Kg

OVEN TEMPERATURE EQUIVALENTS

Fahrenheit Setting	Celsius Setting	Gas Setting
300°F	150°C	Gas Mark 2 (very low)
325°F	160°C	Gas Mark 3 (low)
350°F	180°C	Gas Mark 4 (moderate)
375°F	190°C	Gas Mark 5 (moderate)
400°F	200°C	Gas Mark 6 (hot)
425°F	220°C	Gas Mark 7 (hot)
450°F	230°C	Gas Mark 8 (very hot)
475°F	240°C	Gas Mark 9 (very hot)
500°F	260°C	Gas Mark 10 (extremely hot)
Broil	Broil	Grill

*Electric and gas ovens may be calibrated using celsius. However, for an electric oven, increase celsius setting 10 to 20 degrees when cooking above 160°C. For convection or forced air ovens (gas or electric), lower the temperature setting 25°F/10°C when cooking at all heat levels.

BAKING PAN SIZES

Imperial / U.S.	Metric
9×1½-inch round cake pan	22- or 23×4-cm (1.5 L)
9×1½-inch pie plate	22- or 23×4-cm (1 L)
8×8×2-inch square cake pan	20×5-cm (2 L)
9×9×2-inch square cake pan	22- or 23×4.5-cm (2.5 L)
11×7×1½-inch baking pan	28×17×4-cm (2 L)
2-quart rectangular baking pan	30×19×4.5 cm (3 L)
13×9×2-inch baking pan	34×22×4.5-cm (3.5 L)
15×10×1-inch jelly roll pan	40×25×2-cm
9×5×3-inch loaf pan	23×13×8-cm (2 L)
2-quart casserole	2 L

U.S. / STANDARD METRIC EQUIVALENTS

⅛ teaspoon = 0.5 ml	⅓ cup = 3 fluid ounces = 75 ml
¼ teaspoon = 1 ml	½ cup = 4 fluid ounces = 125 ml
½ teaspoon = 2 ml	⅔ cup = 5 fluid ounces = 150 ml
1 teaspoon = 5 ml	¾ cup = 6 fluid ounces = 175 ml
1 tablespoon = 15 ml	1 cup = 8 fluid ounces = 250 ml
2 tablespoons = 25 ml	2 cups = 1 pint = 500 ml
¼ cup = 2 fluid ounces = 50 ml	1 quart = 1 litre